Life's a Growin' Thing

Ya Grows or Ya Dies

REFLECTIONS ON LIFE AND DEATH

AND OUR TIME IN BETWEEN

Hank Mattimore

Most of the essays in this book were published
originally in the *Daily Republic* newspaper.

My thanks and regards especially to
Amy Honey-McGinnis and Patty Amador
on the *Daily Republic* staff for their
encouragement and support.

Life's a Growin' Thing: Ya Grows or Ya Dies

ISBN 1-931002-49-5

Wordrunner Press, Petaluma

Dedication

This little volume of reflections is dedicated to my late beloved wife, Kathleen Hutchins Mattimore, who with her love and Irish wit was my editor and support as I wrote these essays.

I am also grateful for the encouragement and support of my daughter, Laura, my son, Sean and son-in-law Paul Forgue and to the my friends at the Fairfield Senior Center and all those readers of my column in the *Daily Republic* who have encouraged me to put some of my essays in a collection.

Finally, this book is dedicated to the old Afro-American gentleman, his name long forgotten, who shared with me one of life's great secrets. "Life's a growin' thing; ya grows or ya dies."

Contents

Contents *(continued)*

PART THREE
The World We Live In

Chronicles
A Priest's Story

I'm tooling down the interstate in my bright red Dodge Colt. It's December 1971. "Yippee!" I sing out to the open road. In the trunk of my car, deep in the luggage, underneath two pair of pants, some cutoffs and my one sport coat, lies a black clerical shirt with a worn white collar attached and a pair of black pants. Symbols of my ten years as a priest, I had brought them along "just in case" I changed my mind and decided to go back to the ranks of the clergy. Officially, I am on a six months leave of absence from the priesthood but my gut is telling me that I'm never going back. I'm driving from Florida to San Francisco. Just me. I have a little over a thousand dollars to my name, a car that's half paid for and an MA in education. I'm 36 years old and about to start a new life.

The first time I was conscious of beginning a new life, I was just a teenager." A recent graduate of Fallon High School in Buffalo, I was entering the junior seminary of the Oblates Of Mary Immaculate. For the next nine years, as I progressed through the novitiate and the major seminary in Washington, D.C., my life would be spent in a clerical and religious cocoon. No sex; no women; no money; no decisions. The seminary bells governed our life. The bells summoned us at 5:30 in the morning and reminded us to turn off the lights at 10 p.m. They told us when to go to class, when to eat, when to pray. We wore the same garb, the long black cassock and collar; ate the same food and followed the same schedule. Looking back, it was eerie the way we sort of ghost walked through those seminary years, asking no questions, absorbing, like human sponges, whatever we were taught. While young men our age were starting careers and families, our growth as human beings came to a stand still. While our contemporaries wrestled with paying the rent, we had Oreo cookies and milk breaks.

At the time, it didn't dawn on me that I was living in a twilight zone kind of existence. I felt privileged to be studying for the priesthood and if living in a society without woman, isolated from the world around us, is what it took to become a priest, hey, I was ready. My Catholic family back in Buffalo, N.Y was proud of me, my Dad and siblings honored to have a member of the family in the seminary. I felt special, one of only a very few chosen by God to serve Him. Besides, there was this camaraderie among us, which made our very restricted life style, bearable. We were, after all, young and idealistic, our dreams as big as the world. Like some kind of Roman collar marines, we sort of got off on putting up with the sacrifice of living this very restricted (and celibate) life.

Upon ordination, I volunteered to go to Japan, where I embarked with the zeal of a St. Francis Xavier to convert the "pagans" of Japan to the one, true faith. It didn't take me long to discover that the Japanese were not particularly interested in learning about my Jesus. Little by little, I began to sense that God is bigger than our Christian dogmas. Six years later I returned to the United States, spectacularly unsuccessful as a convert maker and beginning to question my own faith.

I was supposed to return to Japan after a few months' furlough but found myself in 1968 in a country in turmoil. There were racial riots, the assassination of Robert Kennedy and Martin Luther King and a nation at war with itself over the Vietnam War. I volunteered to remain at home and work in an inner city parish in St. Petersburg, FL. While in St. Pete, I started a Day Care Center for disadvantaged kids, two group homes for boys, an inter-racial summer camp and, for the first time as a priest, felt that I was accomplishing something with my life.

What was missing for me and what the clerical priesthood would not allow was the human dimension. I was now 36 years old and, despite my accomplishments, was feeling lonely and unfulfilled. I craved intimacy, a woman with whom to share my life, a family. I hungered for the touch of another human being. It was no longer enough to be a "father." I wanted to be a Dad to my own children.

Years later, friends of mine tell me "Wow! It must have taken a lot of courage to leave the priesthood after all those years." To which I reply, "The truth is, I didn't know what I was getting into." I pretty much knew what I didn't want. I wasn't at all sure what I wanted. In those days, I may have had the veneer of a grown up man but I was still a boy. I had never written a check or slept with a woman. I knew nothing of the world of work or how to hunt for an apartment or what food cost or how to go about getting myself launched into a life so dramatically different from the clerical life I had lived for eighteen years. I felt alternately scared and happy, fearful of the future and confident that I was doing the right thing. Recently, in writing my recollections of my days in the priesthood, I referred to the drive I took from Florida to San Francisco as my "Freedom Drive." Not a bad title.

Blessedly, I had no idea of the adjustment that lay before me. I knew no one in San Francisco, neither family nor friends. I chose to go to the west coast on a whim. On my way back from the six years I had spent as a missionary priest in Japan, I stopped in the "City By the Bay" and was charmed by it. I guess that I wanted to be as far away from St. Petersburg as I could to make a fresh start. What hadn't occurred to me was that I was a popular and successful priest in St. Petersburg. In going from a community where everyone knew me, from a position of respect and status, to being a single, unemployed thirty something newcomer in a strange city was going to be a challenge.

For the first week or so, I played out my adolescent fantasies. After securing a studio apartment in San Francisco, I headed down to Broadway where Carol Doda was doing her bare breast act and the "Green Door" was showing at one of the movie theaters. I recall leaving a strip show where a young college girl gyrated nude on a platform while a handful of lonely men devoured her body with their eyes. The experience left me feeling dirty and persuaded me that spectator sex was not going to fulfill my craving for intimacy with a woman.

3

Within two weeks of leaving the priesthood, I met Lillian at a support group for former priests and nuns called "Next Step." Far from a nun, Lillian was a 26-year-old, vivacious, slightly nutsy Jewish atheist, who helped facilitate groups for Next Step. I went out with Lillian, my first date since my senior year in high school. Two weeks later, this sex starved, very immature priest moved in with his Jewish atheist girl friend. Six months later we were married and within a year had the first of our two kids.

I think my brother married priests will concur that there are few transitions in life more challenging than entering into a committed relationship with a woman after a life of celibacy. Sex was only part of it. I was woefully unprepared to live that closely with another person. My training for the priesthood did not include a course on "Living intimately with a woman." The earthy details were one thing. Good grief! The first time I walked into our shared bathroom and found a bra and panties hanging on the shower door, I knew my life style was forever changed. That small stuff I could deal with but meeting the emotional needs of another person in my life, day in and day out, was more difficult. I wanted her sexually but was not ready to be open to her needs. I had a lot of growing up to do. The celibate life may give you the freedom to be of service to people but there is no guarantee that it wont leave you a dried-up old bachelor sealed off from the joy and the pain of intimacy with another human being.

I soon discovered that if I felt stretched by living intimately with my wife, bringing up kids and the responsibility of providing for a family, stretched me even more. I felt I was being dragged kicking and screaming out of my adolescence, at the tender age of 36. There were consolations. No, much more than "consolations." Being present at the birth of my two kids was a peak experience. Being a Dad to my son and daughter brought out a side of me that had been hidden all those years of being only a "Father." My love for my kids was, and is, "a love that is more than a love." If I should die penniless, the experience of fathering children will always make me feel a very wealthy man.

4

To my sorrow, my wife of almost 20 years filed for divorce back in 1992. I regretted it deeply and still, especially for the sake of my kids, wish with all my heart that it had never happened. I went through a very dark night. A little voice kept whispering in my ear, "Hey, Hank. You blew it again didn't you? First, you bail out on your priesthood. Now you fail in your marriage. Can't you do anything right?"

If there was a silver lining to this painful experience, it did bring me face to face with the God I had left during my years with Lillian. Little by little, I began to re-discover my lost faith. I reconnected with the Oblates at a reunion they sponsored for their former members. It felt good to see some of my oldest and best friends again. In time, I found myself volunteering to help launch a lay associates program for the Oblates and, for a brief moment, even considered returning to the Oblates and the priesthood.

Then, at a support group for persons newly divorced or widowed, I met Kathleen. In time, I knew I had found a best friend, a soul mate, and a person with whom I wanted to share my life. Still, I hesitated , wanting to be sure, when, of course, we both knew that you can never be sure. Finally, we decided to go for it. For our wedding ceremony, we invited Harry Feldmann, a fellow Oblate and former classmate to officiate. He and his wife, Madeline, came out to California for the wedding. Another new beginning.

It's been over thirty years since I heard a person's confession or celebrated Mass or given a sermon in church. The white collar and black clerical shirt that I packed in the trunk of my little Dodge Colt have long since disappeared. Yet, sometimes I wonder if the oils of ordination still remain moist on my hands. Reflecting on my work life since leaving the clerical priesthood, I realize that my entire career has been in the human services. I have been the Director of a community services organization and a Senior Center. I was on the staff of an agency that served people living with AIDS and facilitated support groups for the families of people afflicted with Alzheimer's Disease. I have mentored teenage boys and taught literacy to people in jail. In so many ways, I may have left my Roman collar behind me but not my priesthood.

PART ONE

One Man's Journey

Life's a Growin' Thing

Of all the wise counsels I picked up in twelve years as manager of the Senior Center, none has stayed with me as much as the advice given me by a sage, old black man, a regular at the center. He was telling me that he was probably more active in his retirement years than while he was working. He said, "That's important for me to stay involved with life, you hear what I'm saying, because life's a growin' thing. Ya grows or ya dies."

Think about it. The life we share with plants and animals has that quality of growth. Nature doesn't stand pat. Physically, all of nature is either growing or dying. The old man at the Senior Center was telling me that it's the same for the human spirit, the same for our minds. We grow intellectually, emotionally, and spiritually or we die.

Spiritual growth doesn't necessarily imply frenetic activity. We don't have to be running to every discussion group or fitness class to be in a growth mode. We also grow by quietly reflecting on our lives. We grow emotionally by being more open in our relationships with others. We grow intellectually by reading something more stimulating than the sports page. We can grow as a person by questioning the prejudices we may carry towards people "different" than us and by being willing to forgive those who have hurt us in the past.

One of the most harmful stereotypes that those of us "of a certain age" can buy into is that we are "set in our ways." What a crock! The last half of our lives can be a time of incredible growth. It's a time when we can gather together all the fragments of things we have learned and see the whole picture. It's a time of breaking out not standing pat. Unhampered by the necessity of trying to "prove" anything, we can be free to be uniquely ourselves. Halleluiah! We can change. Life long Republicans can morph into Democrats; racists can decide that human beings are much more alike than unalike. We can expand our hearts to forgive our children, our church, our boss or whomever we have vowed never to forgive.

The afternoon of our life cycle is not some afterthought that our Maker decided to tack onto our lives. It has a purpose. We have a purpose or we wouldn't be here. Your purpose is for you to discover but you can bet that you will never find it by sitting on your hands and closing your mind. "Life's a growin' thing." You'd better believe it.

Some Things I Have Learned on My Journey

Call it life experience or what you will, most of us have learned "stuff" going through life that we wished we knew when we were youngins. Here are ten of my life lessons. You can make your own list but be prepared to change it every few years. As my old Afro-American friend used to tell me, "Life's a growin' thing."

Don't take yourself so seriously.

No matter how important you are or think you are, you do not hold the universe on your shoulders. When you are gone, this old world will keep on turning. Trust me.

Always try to see the big picture.

It's so easy to get yourself all uptight about the thousands of little incidents in our lives that we forget the "biggies." **Health, Family, Friends.** If you have these, it won't really matter much if your name was inadvertently left off the list of contributors to the Boys and Girls Club of East Oshkosh.

Don't waste time with unpleasant people.

Most people are okay. But there are a few whom you will never please. They are determined to be unhappy and there's not a damn thing you can do about it. Avoid them. Life is much too short.

Never hold a grudge.

It ends up hurting you much more than the person who wronged you. Holding grudges and seeking revenge will poison your life quicker than most anything. You don't need it.

Don't live your life in the "Empire of me."

"One" is a lonely number. One of the major paradoxes of life is that the more you concentrate your energies and attention on the big #1, the more miserable you become. Get off your bottom and do something to help others. Remember the prayer of St. Francis. "It is in loving that we are loved; it is in giving that we receive."

Enjoy the moment.

Some folks are always making plans for the future. They talk endlessly about "when the kids are grown, when we have more money, when we retire. You want to shake them and remind them that the only time we really have is now. When we lie on our deathbed, it won't be the mistakes we made that we regret, it will be the trips never taken, the songs never sung.

Have at least one close friend

Whether it's a spouse or someone else, it's important to have at least one person in your life with whom you can be completely yourself.

Make sure you always have younger people around you

The older we get the more we need the vigor and energy of the young. Kids and young folks have a way of keeping us youthful

Have respect for all living things.

Respect for all life starts with yourself and extends out to all human beings and then to all living things. Respect for others helps you to tolerate different points of view and enables you to see some element of good in everyone.

Believe in something or someone greater than yourself

Whether you find your "God" in the redwoods or in timeless poetry or in the First Methodist Church, it's important to acknowledge a spirit that brought us into being out of love and continues to grace our lives.

Showing Up for Your Kids Is Half the Battle

As I write this column, I have on my desk a stack of essays written by teen age kids who are living in Juvenile Hall or in one of the group homes for kids who have no safe and secure home of their own. I'm one of the judges of an essay contest sponsored by the local Juvenile Justice Commission. The kids were asked to write about "The Kind of Parent I would like to be."

A 15-year-old boy (I'll call him Tom) writes, "I'll just want to be there for my kid. My Dad abandoned me when I was little and I feel it would be inhuman for me to put my kid through the same thing."

Michelle, another 15 year old writes, "I want to be there when my children take their first steps and when they speak their first words. Those are the things that make parenting so special. Having a child and being a parent are two totally different things. If you can't see the difference, you are not ready to have a child."

It is no accident that when these wounded kids had the opportunity to write about the kind of parent they would like to be, they wrote about what they missed receiving from their own parents. Their need for their parents to "be there" in their lives is the common thread in all their essays.

I really do have sympathy for today's moms and dads. They live in a complex world and the demands on their time are many. For single parents, especially, it seems that there is never enough time to do the things you have to do. It's just give, give, give all the time. So, I'm not going to lay a guilt trip on you if you have to miss a back to school night or that second grade Christmas play or a soccer game. Just do the best you can. Your kids may not show it but they like to have you there. Showing up is part of your parental job description.

Let me share a personal experience. My grown-up son last played in Little League fifteen years ago. (I still have vivid memories of sitting on those cold benches with other moms and dads sipping god-awful coffee to keep warm.) It always seemed to me that Sean took it for granted that I would be there cheering him on. More than once the thought occurred to me that I must be nuts to be spending three or more hours every week watching my kid play. I could have just dropped him off at the ballpark and picked him up when the game was over.

Then, just last week, Sean called me on the telephone, out of the blue, to say, "Dad, I was just thinking that when I was a kid you never missed one of my Little League games. I just want to say thanks for doing that. It meant a lot to me." His expression of gratitude may have been a tad late but it was sincere and it left this old guy with a lump in my throat.

Just showing up for our kids will not by itself make us good parents or grandparents but, if I am to believe a belated thank you from my son and a bunch of essays written by some kids who did *not* have that experience, it's pretty darn important. Don't you think?

Old Photographs....
A God's Eye View

An old school classmate dropped by the other day with some 1950's vintage photos of our school basketball team. There I am, a skinny, smiling kid, standing there in my basketball uniform, all of 18 years old, fresh-faced and confident, ready for the future.

My son, Sean, cracked up laughing at the skimpy basketball shorts we wore in the picture. Compared to today's style of basketball shorts, sort of baggy and knee length, our trunks looked pretty funny to Sean. I teased him back. By the time you're my age, the styles will have changed again and the baggy shorts guys wear today will amuse the heck out of your kid's generation.

Although Sean had no problem picking out his Dad in the photo, it was obvious that he was looking at a stranger. The kid in the funny basketball togs was no one he knew. I remember having the same experience when I was a kid looking at photographs of my parents when they were youngins. The pictures simply did not look like the Mom and Dad I knew. From my perspective, my parents were people in their late 30's or early 40's, not teenagers.

When I think of photos, my mind goes back to two snapshots I saw juxta-posed at a conference on aging I attended a few years back. The first showed a strapping young Dad with his young boy, wearing only a diaper, riding on his shoulders. Both were obviously enjoying the moment of innocent fun between a father and a son. The second photo showed the same son decades later, carrying his thin and aged Dad, in an adult diaper, on *his* shoulders. The picture was entitled "Father and Son." I stood in front of the photos for a long time, reflecting on the changes that life brings to us all.

The physical changes of aging are so gradual, we hardly notice them happening. We don't *feel* any different because we are the same person on the inside. The kid in the 50's style basketball uniform is me, just as surely as the gray-haired guy that looks back at me from the bathroom mirror today. We change on the outside but the spirit within remains the same. We are who we are. Nothing can take that from us, neither birthdays nor wrinkles nor age spots.

You have heard it said that "pictures don't lie," but neither do they tell the whole truth. The way I see it, you and I are created in the image and likeness of God. As I look at the photo of my 18-year-old self and compare it to the grizzled face I see in the mirror, I am grateful that, at least in the eyes of my creator, I haven't changed a bit.

First Grandbaby

It's grandpa's turn to baby sit. I hold this little nine-month-old miracle in my arms and I know what heaven must be like.

Little Abby, my first grandchild, smiles at me and says something profound like "ga ge goo ga." I swell with pride. "What a smart kid," I say to no one in particular. I bounce her on my knee and her laughter is a tinkling cymbal. I kiss her soft cheeks and play "this little piggy went to market" on her tiny toes. I kiss her again. I can't help myself. I'm a man in love.

My affection for this little baby is way over the top. It's scary. I love her with the same intensity I had for my own kids. It's daddy love part 2, strong, masculine, protective.

No matter how angelic I think her to be, Abby's bodily functions assert themselves. She poops and I clean her up, changing her diaper and putting on her jammies for the night. Then I carry her upstairs to her room humming Brahms's lullaby to her as we go.

I lay her down gently in her crib but this little girl has a mind of her own. She's not ready for sleep, not yet. It's way more fun to play with this outrageously soft touch of a grandpa.

I look at the clock. Wow! It's nine o'clock already. I tell Abby, "Your mommy wanted you in bed by 8:30 at the latest. She just smiles and puts her arms out to be swung around. Can I refuse? Of course not. I'm just a poor male, putty in the hands of this pint-sized charmer of a female.

So, we go back downstairs. I watch the Giants game on TV while she somberly takes my glasses on and off, off and on. Tiring of that, she plays with the buttons on my shirt. This grandpa dude is a source of endless fascination for her.

At 9:30, I cradle Abby in my arms and give her a bedtime bottle. Not even a Barry Bond's home run can distract me from watching my little grandbaby taking her bottle. Her little eyes watch me gravely as she sucks the warm milk into her body. Little by little her eyes close.

Carefully, I carry her upstairs again. This time she hunkers down in her crib for real. I stand over her for a few moments and watch her sleep, wondering if it's possible for a human being to be as happy as I am at this moment.

Somewhere in the world, a war rages, people fight with one another and quarrel over money or possessions or ego. I don't let myself go there now. For this moment in time, this old guy is perfectly at peace.

Oh, I know this season shall pass. Abby will grow up and I'm told by those who have been there, that she will have less and less time for her Poppy. That's okay. It's the way it is. But, in the meantime, I'm going to thoroughly enjoy this dance with my granddaughter. Let the future take care of itself.

Pretty soon, Abby's mom will be home. She will ask me what time I put Abby to sleep and I'll lie a little and tell her it was about 8:30. She'll roll her eyes knowingly. That girl can always tell when I'm fibbing. But she'll thank me anyway.

Isn't that a kick? She thanks me. One day when my daughter is a grandma herself, she will realize that it was I who should have thanked her..

First Smiles and First Poops

My sister-in-law called the other day and man o man was she excited. "Hank, the most wonderful thing happened to me today." "You won the lottery?" "No, better than that," she answered, her voice practically reaching out and shaking me over the phone lines. "Ryan, my little grandson, smiled at me. He looked up at me and gave me his first big smile. He really did. I'm so excited, I could die."

Now other people may not think a baby's first smile is such a big deal but, to a new grandma, there are few things in life more rewarding. I congratulated Phyllis and was honored that she shared this momentous news with me. I was equally delighted two weeks ago when my daughter called me at 10:30 at night to share the news that my granddaughter had actually used the potty for the first time. Halleluiah! The first poop.

Those of you who read this column regularly know that I can take myself seriously at times. I ponder why we have wars and why seemingly good kids go bad and good marriages go sour. I wonder if our country should have gone into Iraq and why we have evil in our world and how can a loving God allow the early death of good parents and let some really bad ones survive. Sometimes, I get so serious about life that I scare myself.

Then, every once in a while, something wonderful happens, like the calls from my sister-in-law or the call from my daughter. For a moment I can put my heavy pondering to rest. A tiny little break through happens in a baby's life and I get a different perspective on life. Wow! A little human being smiles for the first time and I get goose bumps. What a miracle! For the moment, I put everything "important" aside. Sorry about that, fellow Catholics, I know the election of the new Pope is making big news all over the world, and sorry Barry Bonds, I realize that it will be major stuff if you pass Babe Ruth in the home run record books, but your accomplishments just got trumped by a baby's first smile.

Somehow, I don't think I am that unusual. We can get ourselves worked up about the economy or the legalities of gay marriage or the war in Iraq It's good that we do so. We need to pay attention and to add our two cents to what happens in our community and in the wider national and international community. But, at the same time, we care most about our families, our kids and grand kids. It's human nature.

So, I don't apologize for writing to you about a baby's first smile or a granddaughter's first bowel movement because I think you will understand. You have been there, or will be some day, and know exactly what I mean.

Gritting It Through a Final Farewell to a Friend

A Northern California June day. Dressed in the uniform du jour, shorts and T-shirt, I park my car and make my way towards the front entrance of the hospital. The weather is gorgeous but, to tell the truth, I hardly notice it. On my way to visit a close friend who is terminally ill, I'm not looking forward to the visit.

Finding Rick's room, I put on what I hope is a cheerful smile and say something inane like, "Hey, how ya doing?" Rick attempts a smile in return but he grimaces in pain. The truth is, he is not doing well at all. I know it. He knows it. But we both dance around the subject as though death were a dirty word. I ask him if he is able to eat at all. "No, but I was able to get down a little ginger ale." I say, "That's great," as though the being able to swallow a sip of soft drink was something extraordinarily wonderful.

I make small talk. "Kathleen sends her love and oh, I almost forgot. I ran into Bonnie the other day. Haven't seen her in a while. She sends her love, too." Rick nods. I ask him if there is anything I can bring him, like a book or magazine. He shakes his head. "I could bring you a Playboy so you could look at the pictures." He tries to reward my jackass effort at humor with a smile but I see it hurts him to smile. My friend is a very sick man.

I continue the charade. "Do the docs think you might be coming home soon?" A ghost of a smile flits across his face. "I'll be getting out of here soon, one way or another." The implication is clear. He means dead or alive. I choose not to go there. "Yea, this place must be driving you crazy by now?" (He has been hospitalized about six weeks.) His latest complications from the cancer surgery include pneumonia, a flare-up of diabetes and, most recently, a kidney infection.

Rick, whose passion in life is gardening, looks out of his hospital window. "I've seen the trees take on leaves and change color just since I've been in here." I am struck by the sadness in his voice but proceed with my banter. "Yea, another summer has arrived. The days will be getting longer." (What a scintillating conversationalist I turn out to be.) He says nothing.

Recalling that Rick is a dog lover, I chatter on. "Kath and I took a walk over to a Baskin-Robbins last night. We took Coco (our dog) along with us and I gave him a child size scoop of vanilla ice cream. He scarfed it up pretty good, too." The dying man nods his head, as though he gives a hoot. I ask him how his dog is surviving without him at home. With just a trace of self-pity, he answers that "Buddy has probably forgotten me by now." "I doubt that," I say, "That pooch loves you." His face has that far off look as though he were seeing his little dog on his lap in happier times. It's all he has now, his memories.

I've been with my close friend for about 15 minutes now. He is tiring and I am feeling the strain of making small talk with someone who may not live to see another sunrise. I make an effort to get real. For the first time, looking him straight in the eye, I say, "Rick I'd better let you get some rest but I want you to know that I'm pulling for you." I'd like to say, "I'm praying for you" but Rick is not a religious man. I also want to say "I love you," but the words catch in my throat. Too emotional? What a crock of manure that is. I just don't have the balls to tell this marvelous man that I love him. Maybe it will open us both up to tears, to express our real feelings. Instead, I tell him to "hang in there." That's a nice safe expression. I take his cold hand in mine and squeeze it lightly. "See ya, guy."

I leave the hospital and walk out into the warm June sunshine relieved to have put this duty behind me. But I'm mad at myself. I could have done much better. I could have told Rick how much his friendship meant to me over the years. I could have given him permission, through the words I spoke; by the way I acted, to talk about his own feelings as he lay dying in the sterile hospital bed. Instead, I talked about the weather and my dog.

On my way home, the words of the Neil Diamond-Barbara

Streisand duet runs through my mind, "We learned how to laugh and we learned how to cry, so you'd think I'd have learned how to tell you goodbye." Too late. The tears came.

When Your World Turns Upside Down

Shortly after my wife and I returned our trip to Spain, we found out that the cough she had developed on the trip was not just a bad cough. She had the fourth stage of a very aggressive lung cancer. Her oncologist is a compassionate man but believes in being honest with his patients. "Patients with this type of cancer have about a 50-50 chance of living for a year. Statistically, less than five percent live for as long as five years.

Bang! One day we are planning our next trip. The next day we find ourselves in a world grown cold and ominous and very temporary. Those of you who have been through a like experience know what I am talking about. All the stages of grief sort of run over you all at once. You're in denial one minute. Then, you're whining, "Why me?" The next thing you know, you're on your knees bargaining with God. The road to acceptance is not for sissies.

Chemotherapy, the only medical option open to her at this stage in her illness, is not for sissies either. The side effects of her treatment leave her feeling nauseous, very tired and in no shape to jog around the block (or even the house.) Chemo is an equal opportunity killer, offing the body's good cells along with the cancerous ones. Maybe the toughest part of the chemo regime is knowing that it is not a cure. Barring a miracle, all we can hope for is a little more time to live and, at best, a temporary remission of the cancer.

Kathleen, gutsy woman that she is, has managed to find a bright side to the experience. "It has changed my perspective in so many ways." She says. "Because I know I don't have much time left, I am enjoying the important things much more than I ever have." She has become closer to her kids and grandkids. Kath and I have become closer too, realizing, acknowledging the value of the

24

time we have left. "In a way," she muses, "this horrible disease has become a gift."

Always someone who planned carefully ahead, she had her twenty-five year financial plan all worked out. She laughs at herself now and is quite happy having a premium glass of cabernet with her meal and paying extra for a fine dining experience instead of settling for dinner at Denny's.

The most significant change for both of us has been in the realm of the spirit. We have always gone to Church but our relationship with God and the way we look at life has changed. Kathleen has been overwhelmed by the number of friends who have been praying for her. The pledge of prayers has come from the most diverse sources, like her Hindu doctor, Maryknoll Missionaries, friends of her gay son, former priests, developmentally disabled folks I used to work with, men in prison where she volunteered, my tennis buddies, women in her book club, my two-year-old granddaughter. The list goes on.

We both believe in the power of prayer and that prayers are *always* answered. Kath's Hindu physician told her "You know something? We doctors sometimes think we know everything. We don't know anything. When God is ready for you, God will call you."

I'll Take You Home Again Kathleen

So it's come to the 11th hour. My wife, my lover, my best friend is dying. The cancer that had grabbed at her lungs has now spread to her brain. At the hospital, she could no longer hold down her food or even drink so, as a family, we decided to enroll her in Hospice and take her home to die. Here at home, she can look out over our garden and, surrounded by her family and loved ones, make her passage to another life. It sure beats the heck out of a sterile hospital room.

Reaching a decision to withdraw her feeding tube was made much easier because Kathleen had made her wishes known to me and put it in writing to her doctors. She did not want to be kept alive by machine. Her children and I all supported her wishes. That was all there was to it. We all knew that quality of life is very important to Kathleen. Nobody wanted this wonderful woman to have to be in pain or physical discomfort a moment more than she had to.

The Hospice folks are extraordinarily helpful. While being thoroughly professional, they manage to bring something extra, a sense of hominess and warmth. The hospice team reminds me of someone's old Aunt Hazel. You know what I mean? Most families have one, the kind of person who comes into your life brimming with common sense and good humor and puts everyone at ease. The nurse trains us how to give the necessary medications and prepares us for what we might expect in the days ahead. The aide comes by to change her bedclothes and freshen her up. She gives Kathleen a sponge bath while Kath's daughter tenderly massages her mom's feet. All are extraordinarily compassionate and respectful.

As I write this late at night, Kathleen seems to be relatively pain free. Is she really free of pain? I don't know. I hope so. Once in

26

a while she lets out a moan and one of us administers morphine for the pain. When she becomes very restless, we give her Ativan, an anxiety medicine. Her kids and I are with her always. Even at night, there are always two of us watching with her, holding her hand, praying with her. I even sing to her "I'll Take You Home Again, Kathleen," and her favorite ("Amazing Grace") and read from the meditation book she likes so much. We all take turns having our private moments with Kath. Our conversations are pretty much one way because she is unable to respond but it still feels good just to tell her that we love her and say our personal farewells.

It feels like time has stopped for all of us during this time. Her kids all have taken off from work. Friends and neighbors drop by with casseroles or other comfort food. The telephone rings often with friends expressing their sorrow and asking us if there is anything they can do. Her four children and myself are in a kind of time warp. None of us is functioning very well mentally. What energy we have is devoted to caring for Kathleen. My daughter, Laura and little Abby drop by to bring us sandwiches. My granddaughter, at all of 2½ years is way too little to understand what is going on, but her child's laughter and energy are a welcome respite from the grief we adults are feeling.

Today we are beginning the seventh day of our vigil. All of us have thought at one time or another to give Kathleen an overdose of morphine and end this agony but we are acutely conscious that we could not live with that kind of guilt. Her life is in God's hands now. Our job is to stay by her side, to love her, to pray for her, to be present until a loving God takes her.

P.S. The angels came for Kathleen the day after I wrote this article.

Mystery Trip:
A Gift From My Kids

Ijust returned from a "mystery trip," hosted by my kids. Our destination, kept secret until they handed me my boarding pass
at SFO, was a Mexican villa overlooking the Pacific near Puerto
Vallarta. My two kids, son-in-law Paul, granddaughter Abby and
myself, stayed for a week in decadent splendor in a spacious white
marble house, complete with a staff of three and a private swimming pool.

My kids had promised me a "mystery trip" to celebrate my sev-
entieth birthday a few months back but had to postpone it because
of my wife's illness. When Kathleen passed last month, this seemed
a good time for all of us to get away for a while but they did insist
on keeping the destination a secret to pay me back for the mystery
trips I used to take them on when they were little.

We had the villa to ourselves with our own cook serving up
delicious meals, a maid to clean up after us and another staff person
to keep us in lemonade and beer. I have no idea what all this cost.
(I'm not sure I want to know) although Paul assured me these were
off-season rates and a week at a nice hotel would have cost about
the same. Hmm! Maybe.

Anyway, to say that the trip was therapeutic for me is to under-
state the experience. It was not so much the elegant surroundings
in which we stayed or the way we were waited on hand and foot.
To be honest, I would have been content to stay in a rustic camp-
ground as long as I was surrounded by my kids and little Abby. The
luxury in which we spent the week was frosting on the cake, and
this frosting was lathered on with love and a desire to comfort Dad
in his grief.

I wanted to say to them "You didn't need to spend all this money on me," but I didn't because to say so would be to belittle the

gift and the love with which it was given. So I just accepted their generosity with all the gratitude my heart could muster, and said "Muchas gracias."

I read somewhere that when a person is grateful, it's almost impossible for him to be unhappy. I believe that. Anyone who has lived a few years knows only too well how elusive is that thing called happiness. Life doles out the good and bad moments to us. If we are wise, we will be grateful for the good times when they present themselves and grateful especially to the people who make it possible.

So, this lucky old guy spent a delicious week in a private villa high on a hill overlooking the ocean. I watched the graceful pelicans in flight and a young man on the rocks below casting his line into the sea. I listened to the music of the waves lapping against the shore and the sound of thunder heralding the approach of a summer storm. A football field distance away, my eyes feasted on the vision of a school of dolphins breaking the water with playful abandon.

Of course, all this won't last. Now I have to go figure out how I'm going to spend the rest of my days without my sweetheart and best friend. But that's later. For now, I hold in my heart the memory of this trip. I know only that I am grateful for the love that I have received. "Estoy contento." I am one happy dude.

Single Again

This is my third go-around of being a single. My longest stint was the 18 years I spent as a celibate seminarian and Catholic priest. My first marriage, at the age of 37, lasted 20 years, followed by a second bachelor stint of seven years, then my marriage to Kathleen, which ended with her death just recently. So, I find myself at the allegedly wise age of 70 giving the single life yet another shot.

According to my married buddies, the blessings of bachelorhood are legion. I can eat at whatever time I want and whatever pleases my personal palate. I can wander around the house in my underwear when the weather is hot, choose my own kind of music to play, my own television programs to watch, go to bed at a time I choose...all without feeling that I have to please anyone else in the bargain. AND I can throw away my "Honey Do" list forever. Such a deal!

Such a deal! Such a schmeel! Sure I am free and independent. I can let the bed be unmade, drink directly from the milk carton, watch all the baseball games my heart desires, leave the toilet seat up. But you know something? I'd trade them all in for the smell of a woman, for the comfortable feeling of snuggling next to the one I love. Staying up late at night watching some vintage John Wayne movie is no substitute for the warm, satisfying feeling of being able to share my day with some nice pillow talk with my honey before drifting off to sleep.

In the musical "My Fair Lady," Rex Harrison waxed eloquently about the disaster women bring on the male of the species in that wonderful song "Let a Woman in Your Life." But in the end, he too succumbed to the charm of Eliza Doolittle. The truth is, much as guys complain to their buds about how impossible it is to understand their wives, most of us are lost without them.

At our age, it's definitely not just about sex. Besides, in today's world, a single guy (or a single girl) can have all the sex he desires. No, what draws guys to the female of the species is our need for intimacy, our need to love and be loved by another person. We strive all our lives to accomplish things, to be successful in our line of work, to be acknowledged by others but, down deep, it's achieving intimacy with a life mate that makes everything else lame by comparison.

I should add (even if it seems obvious) that singles can attain intimacy with siblings or close friends outside of marriage and that, anyone who has been married can tell you, marriage is no guarantee of intimacy. When a couple is not communicating with one another, there is no lonelier place than the marriage bed. But, all things being equal, I'd rather be married (to the right person) than not. The Holy Book has it right. "Man was not made to be alone."

Does that mean I'll be in the market for a mate anytime soon? Nah! It's way too early for that. But when the time comes, it's cool to be an older male with the ratio of females to males stacked in our favor. I have a tennis buddy, newly widowed, who went looking for dates on the Internet. I kid you not. He had dinner with 30 different women within the next two months. Every other night, he had a dinner date. Finally, completely exhausted and probably broke, he called off the computer chase. Two weeks later, he ended up settling down with his former wife's best friend. She lived across the street. Go figure.

PART TWO

Reflections on Life

People Are More Alike
Than Unalike

I feel fortunate to have shared my brief moment of time on earth with a wide variety of people. Raised in an Irish-Catholic neighborhood in Buffalo, N.Y., I have lived in a fishing village in Japan and studied at a University in Manila. I was a white priest in an Afro-American parish in Florida. I've worked with young children, troubled adolescents and with old folks. As a priest, I have heard the confessions of the very wealthy and the impoverished, the innocent and the cynical. The mother of my two children is Jewish but I have also numbered Moslems among my friends as well as gays and lesbians.

Yet, when I reflect on the diversity among my friends and acquaintances, it's not their differences that I recall. It's their common humanity. Nothing sums up my sentiments better than the words of Maya Angelou, that very wise senior lady who read her poetry at President Clinton's inauguration. "Human beings are more alike than unalike, and what is true anywhere is true everywhere."

It sounds so trite, Pollyannaish almost, to say that we humans are all alike in our yearning for respect and acceptance, that we all dream dreams for our children and desire, so passionately, to love and be loved. But these are the great universals that overshadow our differences.

Oh, we have our individual characteristics all right. Life is not the same for a gay man as it is for someone who is straight. Not the same for an old person as it is for a kid, a Japanese as it is for a Mexican, a bag lady as it is for a banker.

Yet, my own experience will not let me forget that underneath the veneer of color, religion, race or gender, we are much more "alike than unalike." What we look like or who we believe in or how much money we make are all laughably trivial when compared to our own common humanity. It's this likeness we share that makes it difficult to hate a fellow human being without first hating yourself, or to love another person without first loving yourself. We're all in this together, Mates.

Deep Summer and
the Meaning of Life

My Dad always referred to early September as the "Deep Summer." The kids are back in school. The late afternoon sun casts its long shadows on our fields, reminding us that the days are growing shorter. The smell of autumn is in the air.

In California where I make my home, we console ourselves that we still have a couple of months of warm weather ahead of us but the days of summer are numbered. I remember as a kid being a bit impatient to get back to school after that long summer vacation (although it was against the kid code to admit this to my parents.)

At this stage of my life, summer has gone by all too fast. Like a visit from an old and dear friend, I want summer to linger. Surely it can't be time to say goodbye to ice cold lemonade and backyard barbeques and baseball and languid July afternoons that go on forever. Why, the Memorial Day weekend was just a couple of weeks ago, wasn't it? It's almost October you say? Nonsense! Someone has made a mistake.

My late beloved Kathleen used to measure her life not by the calendar but in summers. Her sadness at the waning of another summer was palpable. "I wonder how many summers we have left?" she would say with uncharacteristic mournfulness. For Kathleen, the answer came all too abruptly but most of us avoid even asking the question. Death is not one of the hot topics of discussion at social gatherings.

Still, I suspect that the sunset of another summer gives many of us pause for reflection. At least for me, it's "meaning of life" time. I take out my journal wand write and think deep thoughts. I usually look up some friends I have lost contact with, give my brothers and sister a call, tell my kids I love them. Sometimes, I'll get down on my knees and thank God for all the blessings in my life. For me the end of summer brings with it a desire for closure, like I need to have my house in order before the winds of autumn arrive.

The good Book says, "We have not here a lasting city." That should be pretty obvious, especially to those of us who have been around a half-century or more. Alas, we are prone to keep thoughts of our own mortality at arms length. It takes the loss of a loved one or a close friend or the end of another summer to remind us that life, like the lazy days of July and August, goes by all too quickly.

Magic Happens When the Giving and Receiving Become One

I find myself re-reading *Tuesdays With Morrie* for the third time. What a marvelous read! For those of you who have not read it, *Tuesdays With Morrie* is the story of an old professor, dying of ALS, spending his Tuesdays with a former student, sharing with him some of life's great secrets. Despite his weakening condition, Morrie takes the time to talk, not only to the young man, but to many other people who come to his house with their problems.

At one point in the book, the dying man asks his former student, "Why do you think it's important to me to take the time to listen to other people's problems? Don't I have enough pain and suffering of my own? He answers his own question. "Of course I do, but giving to other people is what makes me feel most ALIVE. When I give my time, when I can make someone smile after he was feeling sad, it's as close to healthy as I ever feel."

I think most of us can relate to Morrie's desire to feel ALIVE. We go to fitness centers or buy new clothes so we can look better. We leave the house and go on a trip to get out of our rut. We re-arrange the furniture or plant a garden or get ourselves a tummy tuck or a Viagra prescription so we can prove to ourselves and to others that we may be old but we're not dead. All these behaviors are very natural and perhaps helpful but I suspect that none of them are as effective as Morrie's formula for feeling really alive, giving something of ourselves to other people.

It's hardly a new idea. Who has not been touched by the Prayer of St. Francis of Assisi? You know, the one that goes "It is in giving that we receive, in loving that we are loved etc." But we forget, get preoccupied with ourselves and our own issues. We're afraid to give of ourselves lest someone take advantage of us.

I recall talking to a recently retired man a while back who

admitted to me that he was bored with life. I suggested to him that he considered volunteering. "Oh no, not me," he said emphatically. "Whatever I do, I want to get paid for it." He preferred being bored to, in his words, "being a sucker and working for nothing."

Morrie didn't think he was being taken advantage of by people who sought his counsel even as he lay dying. The professor was wise enough to know that he needed them as much as they needed him. We are built that way, we human beings. Despite our illusion of independence, we need one another. We need to give and to receive. The magic happens when the two become one.

A Monastery Visit —
Soak in the Silence

The silence is overwhelming at first. Only the songbirds and the whisper of the wind blowing through the cottonwoods breaks the stillness of the morning. I'm thinking, it's wonderful to get away from it all but the abrupt leap into total silence is unnerving. I'm having second thoughts about this idea of taking a four day vacation in a Benedictine monastery.

Located in the high desert area, several miles east of Los Angeles, St. Andrew's Abbey is not your typical destination resort. No swimming pool or golf course here. No nightly entertainment or video arcade. No bar. Good grief! What am I going to *DO* here for four days?

On my arrival, one of the monks welcomes me warmly and gives me my key to a very basic room. It has a bed, a bath and shower, a desk and a chair. No telephone or computer hook-up. No television set.

Ensconced in my spartan quarters, I look over the daily schedule of events at the Abby. They include the chanting of the divine office in the chapel at various times of the day, beginning at 6 a.m. and ending with evening prayers at 8:30 p.m. Real party animal stuff.

I and my fellow guests (there are ten of us as guests at the monastery) are free to attend and participate in the prayer life of the monks as we wish. Three meals a day are provided in the monastery refectory. We eat plain wholesome food and plenty of it. Breakfast is always eaten in silence and guests are requested to follow the monastic practice of the "grand silence" from evening prayer until after breakfast the following morning.

We don't need our watches or alarm clocks. The mammoth monastery bell calls us to meals and prayer services as it has done for centuries in Benedictine monasteries.

At lunch, I find myself sitting across from a fresh-faced young woman, a Baptist, who is going to Siera Leone soon with two other church members to set up a children's orphanage. Laura has a beautiful smile and laughing eyes, not one of those deadly serious, holier than thou types. Far from it. She is just a beautiful young person, fully aware that she is going to one of the most dangerous places on the planet but wanting with all her heart to do something that has meaning.

Sitting next to Laura is a man in his mid-thirties who has been making a good living in the food service business in L.A. I saw him arrive in his beamer convertible. Tom is a good looking guy and obviously successful but he wants something more from life. He tells us that he is staying for two weeks at St. Andrew's with the idea that he might enter the Benedictine Order as a monk. I feel sort of intimidated by Tom and Laura but soon find that most of the other guests are just folks who feel the need to get away for a while from our noisy world.

It doesn't take me long to get into the rhythm of a monastery day. I don't miss at all the 6 o'clock news with the detailed account of all the bad things that happened this day. I don't miss television or the telephone or the sounds of a world that has forgotten how to be still. It's the very stillness that, after a while, is so sweet.

I grow to love the silence and be soothed by it. I enjoy participating with the monks as they send their ancient prayers heavenward. It seems so marvelous that there exists a place where holy men are praying round the clock for the likes of you and me and for world peace and families and people who are homeless and unemployed and for children who are hungry. Something about these men living a life of prayer in the desert just a few miles from the glitter of L.A. makes me hope for the future.

Going to a monastery for a vacation is not for everyone. I definitely would not recommend it for families. ("Dad, Mom, There's nothing to DO here.") But, it you ever feel a longing for quiet and reflection and can do without the need to be entertained, try walking in the shoes of a monk for a few days. It's like a bath for the soul.

Impromptu Banquet
at a Train Station

I have about 45 minutes before my train is going to leave from Union Station in Los Angeles and decide to get me a slice of pizza from the fast food bar. The tables are all taken so I ask a woman sitting alone if she would mind if I shared her table. The woman, who happens to be Afro-American, graciously makes room for me. A minute later, we are joined by a young white kid. There we are three strangers in the most casual of settings.

The young man and I start to wolf down our pizzas when the woman stops us. "Wait," she admonishes us. Then, she spreads out a napkin in front of each of us, giving the illusion of place settings. Surprised, the kid and I watch this woman, a complete stranger, morphing herself into a charming hostess. She reaches out a hand to each of us, bows her head, and says, "Lord, we are blessed in this country of ours to have enough food to eat, we want you to know that we are grateful. Thank you, Lord. Amen." She beams at us. "Now, we can DINE together as brothers and sister."

We didn't have much time to engage in conversation but it didn't matter. The Afro-American woman had already communicated her values. Number one, she was colorblind. She saw us as brothers, not as strangers and had reached out to us with warmth and hospitality. In doing so she made the lonely setting of a train station a little less lonely. Her gesture of putting napkins in front of us and saying grace transformed a junk food meal into a kind of communion.

The experience at Union Station happened to me about six years ago now but it will always remain with me. Where in the world did this woman come from? There have been a number of books written about angels recently. I have tended to scoff at this stuff.

43

But this woman was like an angel to me. Out of nowhere she entered my life and made me feel a connection with two human beings who would have remained complete strangers to me. Her actions spoke to me, louder than any preacher on Sunday morning, that saying a prayer of thanks, even for a dried out piece of pepperoni pizza at a railroad station, transforms the meal into a feast and makes us conscious that in God's eyes, there are no strangers.

Nurture Your Friendships

It is said that a person is fortunate if he or she has a half dozen real friends throughout a lifetime. I believe that. Most of us have hundreds of acquaintances but real friendship is rare.

Think about it. How many people are there with whom you can strip away the masks we all wear and be yourself, warts and all, wounds and all. How many people would you trust with the information that you had cheated on an exam or stolen money or had an affair? How many accept you unconditionally without expecting you to be perfect? There is a reason real friends are rare.

A close friendship with another human being is a gift from God. It enables us to accept and be accepted for who we are. With a friend, we share our hidden longings, our deepest secrets, our "shadow side" because we trust our friend at a level we dare not go with mere acquaintances,

Friendship goes beyond "acceptance." Friends support one another, laugh and cry with one another, get goofy, act weird, rejoice in our little victories as though they were their own. True friends share an intimacy with one another that is rare in life. Someone described intimacy as "in-to-me-see." Not a bad description of real intimacy. Only close friends can trust another person enough to invite him inside his soul.

Friendship knows no boundary of age or gender or race. During this past year, I, this Irish Catholic, former priest, lost my best friend, a Polish-born Jewish professor, 18 years older than I. How do you explain that kind of thing except to acknowledge that friendship has a way of transcending background and beliefs and all the other stuff that we foolishly allow to divide us. My friend's passing did serve to remind me again of the transitory nature of all our relationships. The pity is, if a friendship is lost, not due to a friend's death but because we have let it die. Your friend moves away; you take different career paths; whatever the reason, you lose track of someone who was a real soul mate. You let yourself "fall out of friendship." Ah! That's a shame.

If you don't mind some codgerly counsel, don't let that happen to you. Hold on for dear life to your real friends. There are few things in life more precious.

Can Intimacy Heal?

Can intimacy heal? "Absolutely," says Dr. Dean Ornish, a California physician who gained a world wide reputation by devising a low fat vegetarian diet that seems to work wonders for heart patients. Now Ornish is saying "By all means keep to the veggie diet and do your meditation and exercise but there is a factor even more important than these." In his best selling book *Love and Survival*, Ornish says "I am not aware of any other factor in medicine, not diet, not smoking, not exercise that has a greater impact on your health and well being than love and intimacy."

Ornish has amassed an impressive array of medical data to demonstrate his convictions. In one study of heart attack survivors, those who lived alone were found to be twice as likely to die within a year as those who had significant others at home with them. Another study asked women whether they felt isolated. Those who said yes were almost four times as likely to die of cancer in the coming years than those who did not feel isolated. Another survey of heart patients found that those who answered "yes" to the question "Do you feel loved?" has 50% less arterial damage than those who answered no.

Do studies like this PROVE that love and intimacy heals? Nah, probably not, yet the data supports what many of us have experienced in our lives. As I read Ornish's book *Love and Survival*, I was recalling a conversation I had with an 80 something guy at the senior center I used to manage. "Hank," he told me, "as you grow older you'll learn that there is nothing more important in life than loving someone and being loved in return."

It's interesting to see the medical establishment is finally taking seriously what that gentleman knew instinctively. We are social animals. How we relate to others, the friendships we nurture, the people we feel close to all have a powerful affect on our immune system. Who hasn't discovered that we are more likely to come down with a cold or the flu when we are feeling lonely or depressed? Who hasn't experienced the therapeutic value of a hug or a kiss from a loved one?

Victor Frankl, a Jewish doctor imprisoned in Dachau during the holocaust, remarked that the ones who managed to stay alive through the horrors of this camp were the ones who felt they had something or, more accurately, "someone" to live for. They had loved ones at home, children, husbands or wives, friends who cared whether they lived or died.

What has all this to do with you and me? Look at it as a gentle reminder that it's time we counted the quality of our friendships as important to our health as the meds we take. Maybe it's just as healthy for us to guard against isolating ourselves from human companionship as it is to avoid those high cholesterol foods. Just maybe, reaching out to someone in need is as crucial to our well being as working out at the fitness center. This is hardly new stuff. The power of love to heal is as old as human kind, as old as the power of a mom's kiss on her child's "boo boo" to make it better. It's just that sometimes we forget. Thank you, Dr. Ornish for helping us to remember.

A Sermon From the Redwoods

I stood eyeball to eyeball with a giant California Redwood yesterday. I reached out and touched its rough, macho bark, sensing its life throbbing within. I knew I was in the presence of the sacred. Go ahead. Call me a tree hugger. I don't care. Redwoods just have a way of making me want to fall on my knees.

My own favorite redwood grove is in Armstrong Redwood Preserve in Guerneville. I've picnicked there on hot summer days cooled by the shade of these giants. I've hiked there in the winter when a light drizzle brought to the surface the earth smell of a dampened soil. But yesterday, I saw it at its best, in the lush springtime, with the waters of Austin Creek running high and covered with its carpet of bright green sorrel.

The Armstrong Redwood Preserve has become my retreat, a place of quiet where I can regain perspective on life. I gaze in awe at these 300 ft. tall monarchs, some of them dating back nearly 2,000 years and suddenly I "get" that my lifetime and yours are but blips in time. The redwoods were here when the Magna Charta was signed. They were adolescents when the Europeans first set foot on this soil. Some were living things when a poor Jewish carpenter told us to love one another.

Now I have to admit something to you. Yesterday, when I was all by myself, nose to nose with that old redwood tree, I went over the top. I started talking to it. I asked the ancient one to share its wisdom with me. "How come you guys have managed to stay around so long?"

Well, the old tree never answered me directly but just being in its presence reminded me that one of their longevity secrets lies in the way the redwood trees sort of stick together. The roots of the tree I was engaging in conversation were connected with the roots of dozens of other redwood trees. Contrary to what you might imagine, these tallest of all living things on earth , don't have deep roots at all. They have a very shallow root system but manage to support their great height by this inter connectedness with the other trees in their grove.

Now if I were still a preacher, I'd thank those ancient trees for giving me the seeds of a fine sermon. Don't you think?

Happiness in a Bottle

Hey, it's no longer enough that we Americans have the right to life, liberty and the <u>pursuit</u> of happiness. Now, according to the editor of *The Futurist* magazine, Edward Cornish, we soon will have the right to <u>attain</u> happiness. In our brave new world, says Mr. Cornish, "People who claim that they have not yet attained happiness might receive a subsidy (bliss stamps?) so they can have access to drugs, electrical stimulation, genetic transplant or whatever else they require to achieve happiness." How do you like them apples? Bliss stamps to go along with our food stamps. We want to make sure not only that no one goes hungry but also that no one is unhappy. Hopefully, the editor of *The Futurist* had his tongue in cheek when he was holding forth on people's right to experience happiness. Although, with the multi-million dollar market already booming for pills like Prozac and Zoloft, maybe he was dead serious. Not me. Not for a minute. To me, real happiness is way out of reach of the chemical manipulation of our cells. Not that popping a Prozac may not temporarily ease your anxiety and therefore make you less unhappy. It's just that, for me, deep and lasting happiness is a state of the soul at peace with itself, not some artificially induced biochemical state.

Happiness is the most elusive of our desires. Now you see it, now you don't. I can go along content with my lot until someone asks me if I'm happy. Once I start analyzing myself that way, I don't know if I'm happy or not. Frankly, the question makes me uncomfortable.

I like to think of happiness in small doses, moments of bliss rather than some permanent state of mind. Who in the world is happy all the time? Not me. But I sure treasure those moments.... being present at the birth of my kids, seeing a million stars while standing in a meadow at Yosemite, the pure laughter of a little child, cuddling with a loved one, reading a good book, seeing an excellent movie. You know what I mean. Those are the times you grab on to and enjoy. You do that because you know they are fleeting. Life teaches you that your moments of joy will be interspersed with moments of sadness or difficulty. You can't avoid those moments by taking a "bliss pill" even if Medicare covers it.

The truth is that happiness is pretty hard to define. To analyze it is to kill it. I believe that it has little to do with the amount of money in our checkbook or the size of the house we live in or whether we ever appear on the cover of *Time* magazine. It's much simpler than that and more profound. I like to think that happiness springs from within. When we do the right thing, whether it's stooping to help a child or standing by our mate in sickness or having reverence for life in all its forms, we will no longer have to seek happiness at all. It will have found us.

The Empire of Me

A couple of weeks ago, my son, Sean, told me with considerable pride that he has finally quit smoking. He celebrated his fifth smoke-less month on May 1ˢᵗ. After congratulating him, I asked him what made him finally do it this time (Sean, a smoker since he was 15 had tried and failed several times over the years.)

"Dad," he said, "This time, my resolution to quit smoking wasn't about me. On New Year's Day, I resolved to quit because I knew how worried you and Kathleen are about my health. I wanted to give you guys the gift of my giving up smoking."

Sean went on to tell me that he had been reading Vicktor Frankl's *Man's Search For Meaning*, which is the story of a Jewish psychiatrist's survival in Auschwitz during World War ll. Frankl wrote that, in his experience in the camp, the survivors tended to be the inmates that had something or rather SOMEONE to live for. "All of a sudden, I got it," said Sean, "that the reason these guys survived was for someone they loved," not so much for themselves. I thought I'd do the same thing, give up smoking for you guys."

I was delighted that Sean quit smoking but got even more of a rush that he gave it up out of love for Kathleen and myself. We live, after all, in a culture that is distrustful of people doing things for others. Just take a look at the various Survivor shows on TV The victory is not to the person who is honest and unselfish but to the manipulator who manages to outsmart the other participants. That mentality has seeped into our values. We reward the one who looks out for him/herself first.

They used to call the 70's the decade of the "Me" generation. Seems to me, we have returned there with a bang. How often these days do you hear women actually apologizing on some TV talk show for having put their kids first? What's that about? Then, the guru of the day will utter some kind of pycho babble that goes like ..."It's all right, honey. You didn't know any better. The important thing is that now you have to put yourself first." What a crock!

Women and men too, should BOAST about being unselfish enough to put their kids first or having sacrificed themselves for a cause greater than themselves. These moms and dads deserve a standing ovation not a patronizing pat on the head.

The reality is that when you live only to please yourself, you are setting yourself up for failure. In the long run, it simply doesn't "work." We will accomplish nothing in our lives if our motivation comes only from taking care of what someone has called "the empire of me." We are meant for much more than the personal "stuff" we can accumulate. Trust me, life's real winners are not the ones who end up with the most toys but those who have had the happiness of giving their toys away. The deepest satisfaction in life still comes not from filling up your own Christmas stocking but from filling up those of your loved ones.

Forgiving the Unforgivable

Forgiveness comes hard to many of us. It must have come exceptionally hard to one of the boy soldiers in Sudan. Let me tell you his story. When this kid was seven years old he, along with several hundred other boys, were kidnapped by a rebel army to help them fight their war. The boys were given semi-automatic rifles and taught to shoot. The rebel camp was run with an iron discipline. If any of the boy soldiers hesitated to shoot and kill their enemies, they in turn were killed. There was no choice. You killed or you were killed.

After spending a year with the rebel army, the boy managed to escape and return to his mother in the refugee camp. For several months he was safe there but, one day, the rebel soldiers returned to the camp looking for him. He ran and hid in the garden while the soldiers questioned his mother. The boy could see and hear the soldiers as they talked to her. His mother, trying to protect her son, told them that her son had never returned home since they kidnapped him. The Captain said "I don't believe you," and ordered one of the boy soldiers to kill her on the spot. As the boy in hiding watched in horror, he saw one of the boys beat the defenseless woman to death.

Almost a year later, government troops managed to free hundreds of the boy soldiers and took them to a re-training facility on the edge of the refugee camp. They were given new clothes to wear and watched while their old clothes were burned. The idea was to de-program these boys and help them forget the atrocities they had been trained to commit. At this camp, the boy who lost his mother met face to face with the boy who had killed her. At first his pent up rage erupted and he rushed at the other boy shouting "You killed her. You killed my mother." But then, the hatred he held in his heart seemed to drain from him. The offending boy asked his friend's forgiveness and, incredible as it seems, the two boys hugged one another. That kind of forgiveness seems more divine than human. But it happens.

The older I get, the more I am amazed at the extremes of our behavior. We can be petty and mean spirited one minute and reach the heights of self sacrifice the next. The Good Book says that God has made us only a little less than the angels. Yet, we know from sad experience how hateful and unforgiving we can be to one another.

I knew personally a young man dying of AIDS who had been disowned by his parents because he was gay. When word came to him that his mother was dying and was asking him to come home, the young man refused to go. Steeped in bitterness and hurt, he could not forgive her for rejecting him as her son. The young man's Mom died without her son being there. I felt badly for the mother but even worse for her son. Had he been able to reach down deep in his heart to forgive her, what a liberation he would have felt. As it turned out, he, too, died from the disease within six months. Did he die a happier death knowing that he had paid his mother back for her rejection of him? I doubt it.

I would like to think that all of us are capable of reaching down deep within us for that bigness of heart that allows us to forgive. But, I know too, that there are people who have felt so betrayed, so hurt by life that they are seemingly incapable of forgiving. Some of them will even admit that carrying that burden on their backs hurts them more than it does the person or experience that caused the hurt but it doesn't make any difference. They are trapped by the pain. My heart goes out to them. I wish for them and for all of us that even a small part of the generosity of the boy soldier will rub off on our struggling humanity.

Make Time for the Inner Journey

Travel has a way of changing you, shaking up those brain cells and rearranging them so that you begin to think differently about life. Anyone who has had the opportunity of spending some time in a foreign country knows how exciting and challenging it can be.

But traveling to another country is not nearly as challenging as the inner journey that all of us are called to make sometime during our lives. It's scary to find yourself in a crowded train station in Tokyo trying to find out how you can get back to your hotel but the experience pales in comparison to finding yourself at the end of your days trying to figure out whether your life meant anything at all. That's the journey within that we need to make if we are to make sense of our lives.

Gerontologists tells us that one of the most important things we can do during the final third of our lives is to pull it all together, our experiences, our mistakes, our memories, so that they all add up for us. What did we do with our lives? What was important to us? Who were the people who journeyed with us along the way? Did we love enough? Laugh enough? What lessons did we learn? Did we do harm to others along the way? Can we still ask forgiveness for the things we have done or failed to do? Can we forgive ourselves?

I suggest we could all take a page from the Jews whose tradition is to bring all these thoughts to light once every year at the time of Yom Kippur. At the beginning of the Jewish New Year, they take time to look at the compass of their lives to see if they have gone off in the wrong direction. If they have veered from the right path, they resolve to correct their course for the next year. It's much smarter to take a reading of our lives once a year rather than to wait until the waning years of our lives.

I don't discount the difficulty of embarking on a journey within. Our culture is hardly conducive to quiet thought. These days, not even the library offers a place free of noise. Cell phones and beepers intrude upon our privacy. At home, we let ourselves be distracted by mindless television shows. We run around like chickens without our heads, "doing stuff," and never taking the time to stop and reflect on what it is we are doing. We need to get off the treadmill and reclaim time for ourselves.

During the past few years I have taken to keeping a journal. It forces me to reflect on how I am spending my time, makes me conscious of the time I waste. I recommend the practice to you as one way of keeping in touch with that person within. I know others who meditate daily. A good friend of mine finds rest for the spirit in his fifteen minute morning walk. The way we choose to find our inner space is less important than that we make sure it happens. After all, it's our never to be repeated lives we are talking about. Wouldn't it be a nightmare if we were to reach the end of our days and realize that we were still strangers to ourselves or worse, that we had never really lived?

Goodbye To Youth

Ronald Rolheiser, author of *The Holy Longing,* asks us to imagine that we wake up one morning, look at the calendar, and come to the realization that we are 70 years old.

Whatever else we can say about ourselves, we know for certain that our youth is behind us, gone, dead, caput. All the good diet and exercise in the world, all the face creams and tummy tucks, can never restore the youth we have lost. We can say "Boo hoo. Poor me" to this realization or we can be grown ups and accept ourselves and our time in life.

Happily, while the years of our youth are dead, WE are not dead. In point of fact we are very much alive and, in many ways, we are wiser, more tolerant and enjoy life more now than when we were twenty or forty or sixty, But we are all of these things **as 70 year olds,** not as young people.

I like the author's take on aging. In our society, it seems to me we try so desperately to hold on to our youth, as though it is only when we are young that we are truly alive. That's nuts. I submit that there are only two groups of people in this world who truly savor an ice cream cone or get off on a butterfly or a ladybug, or who welcome each new day as a gift, little kids and their grandparents. The folks in between see bugs. Old folks and kids see miracles.

Rolheiser goes on to say that "Some of the unhappiest people he knows are 70 years old. and older." Then, he adds "It's also true that some of the happiest people I know are also 70 plus." Don't you find that to be true? It's been my experience that the people who cling desperately to their youth, as if in losing their youth, they would lose all that life can offer, are to be pitied. I want to shake them and say "Get over it."

Remember, when we said goodbye to our kids on their first day of school? That was a death of sorts, wasn't it? And when our kids grew up and went to college or when they married? Sure that was

59

the end of that period in our lives but so what? We survived and got on with a new phase of our life cycle. But there is something about the final phase of our lives that makes us dig in our heels and say "Hell no, we won't go." We attack each new wrinkle like an enemy bomber. Every gray hair is an intruder at our gates. When our biggest thrill of the day comes when an acquaintance tells us that we look much younger than our age, it's time to get a life.

We are who we are, warts and wrinkles and gray hair and all. Given the alternative, we are damn lucky to be alive. You can join the ranks of all those unhappy 70-year-old folks if you'd like. It's a free country. Now that I have turned 70, I'm going to hang out with those happy old geezers.

Harnessing the Energy of Love

"Some day, after we have mastered the winds, the waves, the tides and gravity, we will harness for God the energies of love. And then, for the second time in the history of the world, man will have discovered fire."

— Teilhard De Chardin

For me there is something mesmerizing about these words of the scientist/philosopher and theologian, Teilhard De Chardin. As a modern day scientist, he exults in the achievements of science while pointing to a greater energy, stronger than nuclear power, greater than anything we have yet been able to tap. He says, in effect, "Just wait. We haven't seen anything yet. Just wait until the day comes when we harness the energy of love. Then we will have for the second time in the history of the world, discovered fire." That's powerful stuff.

But wait a second, we already know about love, don't we? We know exactly what it looks like. Love leaps out at us when we see a mother caressing her newborn, in the way a newlywed couple look at one another, in the silent vigil of an old man at the deathbed of his wife. We witness love in the self sacrifice of a Mother Teresa and in the way people give of their money and themselves to come to the assistance of the victims of AIDS in Africa. Love is what makes moms and dads put away their savings so that their kid can go to college. It is the glue of long lived marriages, a silent presence at the birth of a child. Love makes a little girl pick up a fallen sparrow and try to nurse it back to health. So what does Chardin mean when he says :some day we will harness for God the energies of love."

What I think he's saying is that we are just beginning to understand what love can do in our world but we're a long way from harnessing its energy. We recognize only dimly that we are one

61

body on our planet, one with fellow humans and one with all living things. Individuals, our prophets, both secular and religious, have grasped the interdependence of human kind with one another and with the environment but it is only recently that the rest of us are coming to this recognition.

We have a long way to go. Most of the time we remain children, fighting one another over our toys. We still need weapons and soldiers and prisons because we haven't figured out a way to protect ourselves without them. It's still an "us" and "them" world where we fight for survival and make enemies of those who could be our brothers and sisters.

Then, along comes this prophet of hope, this scientist/dreamer, to tell us that there will come a time when we become smart enough and brave enough to harness the energy of love. When we do, life will never be the same. Just as when our ancestors discovered fire and, in doing so changed forever the way they lived, so will it be when we truly understand the power of love. An energy will be released in our lives that will turn us on our heads and change the way we see ourselves and all living things.

Pretty idealistic stuff? You betcha! Totally unrealistic? No, because you see the seeds of this all encompassing love have already been planted. Every time I witness an act of bravery or read about some couple adopting six handicapped kids, or some person mentoring a teen or hear of a person donating a kidney so that another person might live, I'm reminded that this vision of Chardin's already exists in the great heart of humanity. All the goodness we see are signs pointing to the day when the vision becomes reality.

Balanced Aging

When I was a young man studying gerontology, we were taught that there were two theories of successful aging. One school of thought pushed the activity agenda. Older people have to keep active and involved with life in order to be happy. Jog, swim, dance, have lots of sex, enroll in adult education classes, learn a new language, volunteer to tutor at your local public school, see the world. You are only as old as you act. Whatever you do, keep yourself busy. If you want to be a happy old guy or gal, keep engaged in doing stuff.

The other way of looking at aging successfully was more mellow. It went something like this. Hey, you have reached your golden years. Now is the time to relax. Take time to reflect, to meditate, to enjoy leisurely strolls in the park (not jogging for God's sake). As an older person, part of your mission in life is to make sense of your younger years. Embrace those gray hairs. You've earned them. You don't have to prove that you are still a tiger in bed or that you can play a mean singles game in tennis. That stuff belonged to your youth. That's not you anymore. Now you can give yourself permission to stop and smell the roses. If you don't do that now when will you do it? This "disengagement theory," as it was called, encouraged old folks to withdraw gradually from the battle, to take to their rocking chairs and enjoy nodding off if the spirit moved them.

Twenty years ago, when I was studying these two styles of aging, the activity theory was considered the way to go. We were taught that the only model of aging worth considering was the go-go one. The most successful older people are the ones who stay busy all the time. Our role model was the woman who had an aerobics class in the morning, led a Great Books Discussion Group in the afternoon and volunteered at the hospital when she wasn't taking that Tai Chi class at the "Y." Our hero was the person who could boast "Why I'm busier now after retiring than I ever was while I was working." In those days, the guys who dared to live a life style that favored quiet days and time to pet your dog, were dismissed as social misfits doomed to loneliness and boredom.

Now that I am on the shady side of 60 myself, I'm not so sure I buy a way of looking at aging that puts so much emphasis on activity. My own theory is that healthy aging has to be a mix of involvement and disengagement. Sure we should keep active. If our only activity is sitting before a television screen watching young people on some mindless "reality" TV show, we are dead already. The undertaker needs to be informed.

But, the activity zealots also need to be called off. Good grief! Didn't we get enough of multi-tasking(even if we didn't have the buzz word to describe it) while we were working or raising a family? We don't really have to be "super seniors," doing everything we did as younger people. That's crazy-making. We are no longer young. Let's get over the charade that we are and start savoring the life we do have. Reading a good book while your cat snuggles on your lap is not a waste of time. It's enjoying the moment. Our gift to the younger generation is to show them how to enjoy life at any age. It's also our gift to ourselves.

Life's Miracles.
Enjoy the Ride

"There are two ways to view the world. One is that nothing is a miracle. The other is that everything is a miracle. I prefer the latter."

— Albert Einstein

Interesting isn't it that a statement like the one above should come from a scientist, not a run of the mill scientist but from one of the greatest scientific minds of our modern era. I think little children get this miracle stuff much better than we do. Did you ever watch a small child's eyes light up at the sight of a butterfly? How about a little kid's delight the first time he or she watches a bubble float in the air or finds a sea shell along an ocean beach? Whatever we jaded adults might think, the kid knows that he is seeing miracles.

Everyday miracles surround us if we have the eyes to recognize them. One of my favorites is the capacity of our memory to store up and recall experiences that happened to us forty or fifty years ago. I find it remarkable that despite all the knowledge and experiences that have been crammed into my memory through over sixty years of living, I can still see that little red wagon I had when I was five years old. I can smell my mom's perfume and my dad's granger pipe tobacco and white owl cigars. I can hear Aunt Kate rattling those rosary beads and Dennis Day singing "Danny Boy" on the Jack Benny show.

Other miracles surround us. Who hasn't read accounts of auto accidents where 100-pound moms find the strength to lift 2,000 pound vehicles off the bodies of their stricken children? But never mind the unusual. Think for a moment of the magical beauty of fields of wild flowers that brighten up our world every spring. Miracles? You betcha!

Just because our world is graced with flowers doesn't make their appearance any less miraculous. Just because a man and a woman can make a baby almost anytime does not make her birth any less wondrous.

I wish I were awake enough all the time to appreciate that miracles that bless my life. Alas, there are times I don't see them at all. I sleepwalk, acting as though I belong to that pitiable group of people who don't believe in miracles at all. What a loss for me.

But then there are other times (I bet you've experienced them, too) when the world seems to come alive before my eyes. I don't drag my feet. I run through those days like a kid with his first kite, forgetting the pain in my hip or the loss of my youth or the money I owe MasterCard. Those are the days I live for, when, as the good Book says, "the kingdom of God is within" and everything is a miracle.

Riches of the Heart

When I want to challenge myself to grow into a better person, I find few authors who can reach me as powerfully as Anthony DeMello, a Jesuit priest from India. He once told a story about an ambitious young husband who was laying out his career plans to his wife. "I'm going to work hard, honey, and someday we're going to be rich." The man's wife looked at him with love and replied, "We are already rich, dear, for we have each other. Someday, maybe we'll have money."

Living in a society that puts such a premium on material wealth, it is good to remind ourselves that what truly makes us rich is our relationships. Our bonds with parents, spouse, children, siblings and friends are our most valuable possessions. The moments when we experience real intimacy with another human being, the times when we feel absolutely free to be ourselves with our close friends or when we relive childhood moments with a brother or sister, or see understanding in the eyes of a friend...these are the riches of relationships that make our material "stuff" seem like nothing in comparison.

I asked a lawyer who had volunteered three years of his life to work among very poor people in Zambia what he had learned from Zambian people. He replied simply, "I learned from them that you can be very happy without having a lot of things." I have talked to countless older people in this country who lived through the great depression and they echo the same sentiments. One couple told me, "We had so little, it was almost laughable. Yet, we pulled together and raised a family." They hastened to add, "It wasn't just a matter of survival either. Those were the happiest days of our lives."

I know that there are those who will dismiss these stories as Pollyannaish. They think to themselves, "Yea! Yea! That's all warm and cuddly, but show me the money. I want to shake them and say

"Don't you realize that no, it's not about money at all. "Money." As a friend of mine used to tell me, "is a handy thing not to be without." That's all. It has its place but we really don't need much of the stuff our money buys, do we? Rich is an attitude of the mind. It's a kiss from your sweetheart, a hug from your grandchild, the satisfaction you get back from giving of yourself to others. Rich is loving and being loved. In the end, it's all about relationships, baby.

Being a Dad is Forever

Did you ever notice that most of the articles written about Fathers' Day are written about young Dads? There are pictures of Dad in the delivery room, or holding his infant daughter or coaching his Little League son, but not a lot about Dads after the kids have left the nest and are out on their own. Yet, Dads, like Moms, are around a long time after their kids have grown up. They continue to be Dads but in a very different way.

As a father of adult children, I sometimes reflect on my own changing relationship with my kids. When they were very young, I was their "god," their hero who knew all things and could do no wrong. As they grew older and smarter, my halo gradually disappeared. By their teen years, I had begun to grow horns and carry a pitchfork. Oh, it wasn't that bad, not really. Let's just say that they were more perceptive in picking out my shortcomings. More than that, the closeness I had with them as little kids began to melt away. At times, during their teen years, I felt that my only possible usefulness to them was as a provider of pocket money and the keys to the family car.

Around the ages of 18 or 19, I could sense a change. While never returning to the rose-tinted view of me they held as little kids, they began to accept me as an "okay" Dad. As they grew out of their own self-absorbed view of the world, I magically turned into a person in my own right. I know I speak for millions of older fathers when I say it's quite a relief being neither an ogre nor a saint to your kids. It's great just being seen as a human being, a fellow adult.

I like this new role. I still love my kids fiercely and want the best for them but I can relax more. It's not all up to me and their Mom to make things right anymore. Maybe it never was. But now I realize that their lives are in their hands. The Little League days are long gone. So are the parent-teacher conferences, the school plays, and the sleepovers with their friends. I'm no longer the one who gives them spending money or who is responsible to put them on restriction if they screw up. For better or worse, I've done my parent thing. Now, it's up to them.

Still, having said that, and rejoicing in my newfound liberation, I know that, for my kids, I'll always be "Dad." I also know that, no matter how many birthdays they have put behind them, they will never be other than "my kids" to me. Being a Dad is forever. I may have felt my role more intensely when they were little, but fatherhood is a bond that transcends time.

Fathering a kid is pretty heady stuff, no less wondrous because most adult men share the experience. The relationship I have with my children is deep and strong and unlike any other relationship. Being a Dad has defined me, changed me, challenged me. It has made me stretch and grow in ways that I could never have foreseen.

I'm not sure I realized all this when I was just a young Dad. But, believe me, all you guys holding your newborn babies; you're in for quite a ride. And yes, take it from an older Dad, it's worth it.

Six Cool Gifts
Our Kids Give Us

In our most overwrought moments, moms and dads can reach a point when we conclude that out parent-child relationship is a one way street. We are doing the giving and our kids are doing the taking. Not true. If we open our eyes a minute, we will notice that the little people in our lives are givers too. For starters, here are six pretty cool presents kids offer us daily.

The first gift — the gift of play

All of us knew how to play at one time in our lives. But somewhere along the line, we contracted an Alzheimer's of the spirit. The world become a deadly serious place and we forgot how to laugh at ourselves. The solution? Learn from the kids how to lighten up. Blow some bubbles, slap around a balloon, kick a beach ball. The kids will show you how.

The second gift — honesty

We didn't start out this way but too many of us have learned to be phonies. We dissimulate and tell lies and pretend we know stuff that we don't, all to protect our fragile egos. Life is easier for kids. If Grandpa has a big nose, the kid will say "Grandpa, you have a big nose." That kind of honesty is refreshing.

The third gift — the gift of tears

This gift is especially valuable for guys. When kids are hurt, they don't feel they have to stuff it. They cry. It's the most natural thing in the world. That's one reason they recover so quickly. Listen to the kids and re-discover the therapeutic value of tears.

The fourth gift— a sense of wonder

When did we last marvel at a butterfly in flight or ask Who created God? There was a time when we were more curious about life.

Remember? Learn from the little folks to ask "Why?" more often. It's the beginning of knowledge and keeps us more alive.

The fifth gift — humility

One of the reasons kids learn at lightening speed is that they are not afraid of making mistakes. No one has told them yet that it is shameful to screw up. I took skiing lessons with my daughter when she was about seven years old. She fell down 20 times to every fall I made. Guess what? She learned to be a pretty fair skier. I made less mistakes but never learned to ski.

The sixth gift — live in the present

I don't know who first came up with the expression "*Carpe diem,*" (seize the day) but I suspect it was first said by a nine-year-old Roman kid. Children live in the present. It's their gift to us adult worry birds who are forever wringing our hands about what might happen five years from now.

Mature Lovers Want
Intimacy First

I hosted a radio talk show one time on the subject of re-entering the dating scene in our middle years. Interesting show. Lots of callers, mostly women. That's hardly surprising since most of the singles in this age group are of the female persuasion.

My callers were pretty clear about their issues. Whether newly divorced or widowed, these women were not ready to call it quits to their sex lives. Their problem was the shortage of eligible males. They also made the point that it's not so much the sex that they miss from their married days. It's intimacy. As one widow put it, "I miss the cuddling, the feel of his body against mine, the touches, the warmth of his love. Sex is not nearly as important as feeling I am loved."

As I listened to the callers, I was wishing that older guys were listening. Guys worry so much about performance in the bedroom. Good grief, pretty soon Viagra will be outselling aspirin at the local pharmacy. It might help the male of the species to be reminded that we are not machines but people, that the women in our lives are far more impressed by the quality of our love than the firmness of our erections. Sex is a human act, an act of love between human beings, not a performance. Hugging, kissing, cuddling, all of these are just as important, maybe even more so, than the act of sexual intercourse.

One male caller had some good advice for the women, too. He admitted that guys are overly concerned with the physical act of intercourse but he added. "You women worry too much that your bodies are not as attractive as when you were 25. I'll let you in on a secret. Men want intimacy, too. Whether or not your breasts are as firm as they once were matters less to me than you might think. Loving and feeling myself loved by a woman is important for me, too."

73

It was only one radio talk show but I felt encouraged by some of the wise comments I heard. It made me feel that maybe men and women are not from different planets after all. At least in our more mature years, some of us "get" that the most important thing in life is to love and be loved and that intimacy trumps sex anytime.

Is *Anything* All Right?

When I think of the late Fred Salsman, a fixture at the Senior Center for many years, an expression he often used when he greeted me comes to mind. Fred would look at me mischievously, cock his head to one side, and say, "Well, is anything all right?" The rest of the world says "Is everything all right?" but not Fred. He wanted to know if *anything* was okay.

Fred's greeting sure puts a different spin on life doesn't it? If we have lived long enough to have a gray hair or two, we know how rare it is to have even one day when *everything* is copasetic. Just doesn't happen does it? On the other hand, even on a day from hell, something will be all right. Good grief, if we are still alive to complain about what went wrong, that's one major thing that went right. Old Fred never asked if everything was coming up roses. He just wanted to know if even one little rose was blooming.

Lord knows, as each decade passes, we all experience our share of problems. Aging. as we've heard "ad nauseum" is not for sissies. Along our path through life, we lose parents, siblings, friends, sometimes even our own children. Our physical powers are not what they once were. Maybe we find ourselves single again late in life, or strapped for money or frustrated that we just don't feel as good anymore. Feeling this way, it's damned hard to pretend that everything is great. We know better. Putting on a front and a smile when we are down doesn't fool anybody very long, least of all, ourselves.

Recalling Fred Salsman's quirky greeting, helps me to put things in perspective. It's perspective that lets us smile at our foibles, joke about our wrinkles and take those gray hairs in stride. It's perspective that helps us to see ourselves and the world around us, neither through rose-colored glasses nor through the dark glasses of unrelieved misery.

Despite our losses, despite that arthritic knee, life is still a hoot, still has its moments of wonder and beauty and laughter. Sweet little girls still sell their girl scout cookies; five-year-old witches and ghosts appear at our door on Halloween; young men and women give their lives for their country; Dads give "horsey back" rides to their kids; grammas kiss the "boo boo" on their grandson's knee, somewhere a couple falls in love and somewhere a new baby cries.

Is anything all right? You betcha it is, Fred. Thanks for asking.

Misfortune Can Be
a Wake-Up Call

On my way to play an early morning round of tennis last week-end, I stopped by a convalescent hospital to visit a fellow-worker. Terry is only 40 but strokes can happen at any age. I went there to help him with his breakfast. The stroke has pretty well incapacitated his right side so he couldn't handle a fork or a spoon very well. His speech was affected, too.

Last week Terry was regaling us with stories of his trip to Alaska. Today, this funny, articulate man couldn't put more than two or three words together without stopping in frustration, unable to verbalize his thoughts. It was painful for me to witness, but not nearly as painful as it must have been for Terry.

I stayed with him while he struggled with his breakfast. The nurse told me to let him do as much as possible for himself so I mostly just sat there, feeling kind of awkward and carrying on a one-sided conversation with a man who could no longer say much in return. It was awful. After Terry had finished breakfast and a decent time had elapsed, I said goodbye, feeling relieved to be out of the sad confines of the convalescent hospital.

As I walked into the brisk, early morning of a California spring day, I let the emotions of what had just transpired wash over me. Perversely, I felt very, very fortunate. I walked on two good legs. Although twenty years older than Terry, I was in good health, on my way to play tennis. I can speak. I can run. I can drive my car. Back in the hospital, a comparatively young man lies in bed unable to do any of these things.

It's crazy isn't it, the way it takes the misfortune of others to wake us up to the gifts we possess. We spend our days fussing over the things we could buy if we had more money or worrying about unpaid bills or complaining about the price of gas and all the time we don't see the forests for the trees. We take for granted that we can smell a rose and taste the sweetness of a ripe apple or hear the laughter of children at play. We too easily overlook the simple pleasure of spending a few minutes in conversation with a friend or singing in the shower.

In Kate Hepburn's memorable phrase, "Life is delicious." Sometimes it takes a visit to a convalescent hospital to understand what she meant.

Actions Speak Louder
Than Feelings

Rabbi Kushner, author of *When Bad Things Happen to Good People*, tells the story of a young couple who asked him to officiate at their marriage. They requested that he change the words of the wedding ceremony from "until death do us part" to "as long as our love shall last." When the Rabbi asked them why they wanted the change, the couple explained, "We would not want to stay together if we no longer loved one another." Shucks! Isn't that beautiful? No it's not.

Kushner, to his credit, turned down their request. He told them that yes he understood that many marriages end in divorce but there is something more important at stake than how they may "feel" about one another in 20 years. "Love, real love," said the Rabbi, "calls for commitment to one another." Commitment trumps feelings anytime just as real love goes way beyond infatuation.

Feelings, it seems to me, have taken center stage in today's culture. For some, feelings have become the sole arbiter of what is right or wrong. If something feels right, it is right.

Not in my book. What makes us truly moral human beings is not how we feel towards one another but how we act.

I recall a woman in a support group I facilitated for caregivers of people living with Alzheimer's disease. Her 90-year-old Mom, while in the final stages of her dementia, had just staged another miraculous recovery from a heart attack. "I was afraid Mom was going to die," said her daughter. "At the same time," she admitted, "I was afraid she wouldn't." She looked at the rest of the group for our reaction, perhaps a little embarrassed at the implications of what she had said. She needn't have been ashamed. Everyone in the group could relate to what she was experiencing. No one knows mixed feelings better than caregivers for people with Alzheimer's.

What was far more important was that she was hanging in there. She continued to stand by her Mom despite her mixed feelings. It's been said that half the battle in life is simply showing up. This daughter may have felt like walking but she didn't.

Rabbi Kushner was making the same point to the young couple on the verge of marriage. Commitment trumps feelings anytime.

A Valentine's Day Story

Kathleen's Mom and Dad had been slipping for some time. They were, after all, in their 80's and poor health was catching up with them. They still lived by themselves but Kath and her sister would take turns dropping in on them from time to time to make sure they had enough groceries and that they were doing okay.

Valentine's Day 1979. My wife dropped by Mom and Dad's house, in the Mission District of San Francisco, to do a quick check-in. Like a good daughter, Kathleen was carrying some flowers as a Valentine's Day gift. She rang the bell but there was no answer. This didn't bother her much because her parents were both hard of hearing. Kathleen had her own key so she let herself in. Once in the house, she called out "Mom and Dad, Are you home?" There was no reply. Getting just a bit anxious now, she went to the foot of the stairs and called out a second time "Mom, Dad are you there?"

Putting the flowers in a vase and leaving them on the dining room table, Kathleen went up the stairs to the second floor. "This is unlike them to be in bed at this time of day," she thought to herself. It was, she recalls, about 2 o'clock in the afternoon.

She called out a third time but no answer. Definitely worried now, she hastened to their bedroom, fearing the worst. The bedroom door was very slightly ajar and, at first, Kathleen thought she heard the radio playing. Heart pounding, she pushed the door open and, to this day, she will never forget the scene that met her eyes.

There on the bed, cuddled together like two young lovers, were her parents. "Mom," Kath recalls was "looking lovingly into the eyes of her husband of 50 plus years and singing softly to him in her own beautiful voice, "Let me call you sweetheart, I'm in love with you." Neither parent noticed their daughter at the door. "Mom and Dad were totally absorbed in one another. I quietly shut the door and left the two love birds alone. They obviously didn't need their "kid" around to spoil a precious moment together.

Kathleen went downstairs and penned a little note to the flowers she had left in the dining room. "Here's a little token gift for you two from all of us. I hope you know that the greatest gift you gave to us kids is the love you have always had for one another. Happy Valentines Day."

Christmas Thoughts

Someone once said that there are places in the heart that you never even know exist until you love a child. I believe that. When I became a parent, I got in touch with a part of me that had never surfaced before. I found myself loving my kids with a kind of fierceness that almost scared me. I am a mild mannered guy, a peace loving man, yet I knew, just as sure as I am writing these words, that I would have killed anyone who hurt my children. Most moms and dads understand what I'm saying because they would do the same for their kids.

I think this strong emotional bond between parent and child is what gives the Christmas story its eternal relevance and power. People, who know or care little about dogma or theology or even for attending church, are swept up in the story of a poor carpenter and his wife and the birth of their baby boy. The story transcends what we know as organized religion and speaks directly to the heart. It's a tale as old as human kind and yet personal to you and me. We identify with Mary and Joseph's joy and share their fears and uncertainly about the safety of their child because Jesus is every child, yours and mine and everyone's.

One would think that with the presence of this strong bond between parent and child that our kids would all be protected and loved and cared for. But looking at our track record as a nation, I'm not sure we are doing very well at all. Otherwise, how do we explain that there are over half a million kids in foster care in this country alone? How do we rationalize the vast number of latch key kids who come home from school to an empty house or the throw away kids that parent kick out of their homes or the crack babies? Why is it that over a million children are being raised by their grandparents?

We have to do better by our kids and "better' does not mean simply loading on the toys under the Christmas tree. All the game boys and Dora dolls can't begin to make up for not being there for our kids. Somewhere along the way, we have, as the Legend of Bagger Vance would have it, "lost our stroke." We have tried to substitute "stuff" for love and it doesn't work, neither for us nor for the children entrusted to us.

A number of years ago, in the midst of a school board election, I remember an old friend of mine, a staunch conservative who was hostile towards any government handouts, surprising me by voting yes on a school bond issue. This was especially puzzling since both his kids and his grandkids were past school age. When I asked him about it, he said simply, "Hank, the way I look at it is that all these kids are our kids." My Christmas wish for you and for me is that all of us start seeing all kids as our kids. Maybe, in doing so we will rediscover that place in our hearts that only the love of children can uncover.

Christmas Gifts From the Heart

The Christmas season will soon be upon us and we will be besieged on all sides to go out and spend, spend, spend. May I suggest an approach more in keeping with the man whose birthday we celebrate. Give the fruit cake to Aunt Tess, the shaving kit to Dad and the video games to your grandson, if you must but try also to make room in your heart for some others who might not have made your Christmas gift list this year.

Call up a local nursing home and find out the names of residents who have little or no visitors. Drop by and say "Hi." Bring along some cookies or a stuffed teddybear. You may get a smile in return or, at worst, a blank stare. That's okay. The important thing is that you reached out to another human being.

For the person who has everything, make a donation in his or her name to the Salvation Army or UNICEF. You can give a donation to Heifer International and they will give a goat or pig or other farm animal to an impoverished farm family in a third world county.

If you have grandchildren, take them with you Christmas shopping, not for themselves but for kids whose parents cannot afford to buy them a lot of presents. Have the kids go with you to the local fire station and drop off the gifts they have purchased.

Renew a friendship with someone you haven't seen in a long time.

Offer to baby-sit for the single mom next door so she can go Christmas shopping or do the same for the spouse of a person with Alzheimer's disease or offer to take someone Christmas shopping, perhaps an elderly person who can no longer drive or a disabled person.

Tell your grown up kids that you are proud of them and surprise them with a big hug.

Ask forgiveness of someone you may have hurt.

Make it a point to introduce yourself to the new neighbor on the block, the one who moved in six months ago and you never had the chance to meet.

Be especially kind to the overworked sales persons at the Mall or elsewhere who are trying to cope with more Christmas shoppers than they can handle.

Let your heart expand to pray for peace in Iraq, for our troops, for kids orphaned from the war and from parents who have died of AIDS, for the homeless everywhere. Pray for kids in juvenile hall and people who will be spending Christmas in hospitals. Hold them all in your heart.

Read the Christmas story, the real one in the Bible, to your kids or grandkids. If there are no little folk around, read it to yourself. You don't have to be Christian or even religious to appreciate the wondrous and touching story of a young couple and the birth of a child. The Christmas story is as old as humankind and as young as a newborn baby.

Nine New Year's Resolutions

That Have Nothing to Do With Losing Weight or Signing Up at the Local Fitness Center

We are getting so entirely self absorbed these days that all we can think about is personal health and fitness. Our New Year's resolutions reflect this self-absorption. How many of us come up with a variation of the following: "I resolve to sign up at the fitness center and this year I will definitely persevere in flattening my tummy and getting my body in shape before summer so I wont be embarrassed to appear in a swim suit." Or, "This year I will go on a (you name the latest diet craze) and resolve to drop at least 20 lbs."

Hey, we are getting to be a nation of lardos so dropping those pounds is a good idea and who can be against working out at the Y or visiting the neighborhood Curves? But, you know something? There is a world out there beyond our bedroom mirror. May I suggest some resolutions that are NOT focused on improving our bods.

Renew your acquaintance with an old friend. Remember Mary, your best friend in high school? See if you can find her and call her up just to say Hi.

Make an effort to understand the younger/older generation. Youngins need to remember that old folks are not all arch-conservative killjoys who are hopelessly out of touch. Seniors need to lighten up on kids, remember what it was like when you were that age and be supportive of the younger generations. We're all in this together, mates.

Forgive someone who has offended you. Forgiveness doesn't really hurt much at all and it will get the monkey off your back.

Do something this year that you have never done before. Take that risk. You don't want to reach the end of your days moaning over what you might have done.

Tell your kids or your parents or your grandparents that you love them and are thankful that they are a part of your life.

Flex your mental muscles. Read some books and magazines that move those marbles around in your brain. Learn a language. Attend a class at the community college. We have more than enough physical fitness centers in this country but not enough resources for our mental fitness. Go on-line or to the library or to adult education class to improve your brain.

Be kind. For heaven's sake, life is way too short to be cursing other human beings or cutting them down by our gossip, or judging them. Let God do the judging. All we need to do is follow that golden rule we learned when we were just kids.

Continue your own personal spiritual journey. We all need to grow whether we are 18 or 88. Meditate, pray, reflect. It's important to re-examine our own beliefs and spiritual values as we age. Remember our old friend Socrates? "An unexamined life is not worth living."

Volunteer your time somewhere. Tutor a kid in school or an adult who is studying English as a second language, be a Big Brother or Sister, visit an oldster in a convalescent hospital, be a foster parent. Volunteer opportunities abound wherever you live. Grab one. Believe me, you'll gain more from the experience than you ever thought possible.

Well, there you have them, nine resolutions that do not include anything about keeping your svelte figure or counting calories. I suspect you'll find that getting your mind off yourself and the way you LOOK will not only improve your health but make you a better person where it really counts, on the INSIDE. Happy New Year.

I Wanted My Kids To Know Me

Writing a spiritual will is a gift both to your family and to yourself.

Recently, an acquaintance of mine had the terrible misfortune of losing his Dad in a car accident. As the only child, it fell to Dan to go through his father's apartment where his dad had lived since the death of his wife three years before. He told me that, as he cleaned out the apartment, he was hoping to find some personal note that his Dad might have left him but, to his disappointment, he found nothing. "I just wanted a note, an old letter, something to remind me of my Dad. I found nothing. It made me feel sort of empty, like I was missing something.

That "something missing" is being provided more and more frequently these days by people who have re-discovered the ancient practice of drawing up a spiritual or ethical will. A spiritual will is a way to share your values with your family in the same way that a legal will provides instructions for passing on your property and possessions.

Some have described a spiritual will as a love letter to your family and friends. In it you have a chance to tell your loved ones what was important to you in life, what you believed in and hoped and prayed for. You can put on paper family stories, ask for forgiveness, relate your most precious memories of them, the way you remember your daughter in her first prom dress and the time your three year old son ran out of the house buck naked. Maybe, you can tell them things about yourself growing up as the kid they never knew, the lessons you learned from life, that special teacher who helped turn your life around.

Most of all, writing your spiritual will is your final gift to the people who have been most important to you. We don't say, "I love you" nearly enough in life. We can let all those inhibitions go when we write our farewell letter. This is your opportunity, the

89

man who lost his Dad in an auto accident, is now writing his spiritual will. "I can't do anything about the fact that my Dad and I never said goodbye but I can make sure my kids will never experience that sadness."

AUTHOR'S NOTE: If you want to know more about writing your own spiritual will, you might find helpful my booklet, *Legacy of the Heart*. Contact me at: hmattimore@yahoo.com

PART THREE

The World
We Live In

Feeding the Wrong Wolf

"Every gun that is made, every warship launched, every rocket
fired signifies in the final sense a theft from those who hunger
and are not fed, those who are cold and are not clothed."

— President Dwight D. Eisenhower, April 16, 1953

I am not a pacifist. If I am under attack, I will fight back. If my
country is attacked, I believe that we, as a nation, must defend
our homeland. That being said, I believe that war is a last resort,
almost always a mistake and ultimately a wasteful and ineffective
way to solve the issues that divide us.

That is why President Eisenhower, by no stretch of the imagi-
nation a pacifist, found himself questioning the wisdom of our
country or any country wasting precious resources on weapons of
war when we could be spending those resources on growing crops,
developing medicines, purchasing school books and making our
world a more peaceful place to raise our families.

War is a kind of madness. We equip our youth with sophisticat-
ed weaponry and send them abroad to kill and destroy young men
and women from a distant country. In the process civilians die,
the innocent suffer, children are orphaned. Ultimately, someone
declares a victory but there are no real winners, only different kinds
of victims. Waging war diminishes victor and vanquished alike.

There is a story told about an old Cherokee grandpa who is
teaching his grandson about life. He says, "A fight is going on inside
me and you and every other person. It is a terrible fight between
two wolves. One wolf is evil. He is anger, envy, greed, arrogance,
guilt, resentment and self-pity. The other is good. He is joy, peace,
love, kindness, generosity and empathy." The young boy thought
for a minute then said to his grandpa, "Which wolf will win?" The
old Cherokee simply replied, "The one you feed."

It seems to me that when we go to war, we are feeding the wrong wolf. And in doing so, we are destroying the goodness within each of us. We are not bringing peace to the world but fostering hatred. We are not feeding the hungry or clothing the naked. We are killing not only our own soldiers but also the lives of innocent civilians. More importantly, we are starving the good wolf within ourselves, the wolf that wants peace for ourselves and our children.

The March 14, 2005 issue of *Time* magazine has a cover story about the number of people (over one billion) who are living in extreme poverty in our world today. According to a United Nation's report entitled "Children Under Threat," more than half of the world's children suffer "extreme poverty." That means families that live on less than a dollar a day, families that don't have save drinking water or enough food to ward off starvation. It means children die because of sickness that could be prevented.

This year we will be spending approximately 500 billion dollars to support our military operations and 16 billion in aid to those who live in extreme poverty throughout the world. Where have we gone wrong?

This is not a Democrat vs. Republican thing or blue vs. red. Letting children starve to death in a world of plenty transcends all that. It's time we revisited President Eisenhower's words and paid attention to the truth that he utters.

"Every gun that is made, every warship launched, every rocket fired signifies in the final sense a theft from those who hunger and are not fed, those who are cold and are not clothed."

Offing Children
in the Netherlands

The murder of children has always ranked number one in humanity's Hall of Shame. We were outraged when the Nazi regime in Germany put Jewish babies to death and when the Japanese put to death infants during their infamous rape of Nanking. Just months ago we were revolted at the sight of Chechnian terrorists rubbing out the young lives of Russian school children.

Now, in the Netherlands, under the guise of "mercy" killing, the Health Ministry is being petitioned to allow medical professionals to put to death newly born children who are suffering from an incurable disease or extreme deformity.

Mercy killing of adults is already legal in the Netherlands but children under the age of twelve were protected, presumably because kids were not capable of giving informed consent to their own extermination. Now, the prestigious Groningen Hospital is asking that the law set these safeguards for children aside. The hospital has gone even further in admitting that they have already carried out a number of mercy killings on underage children. In effect, they are saying, "Hey, we're already putting children to death. Let's make it legal."

People may differ, in good conscience, about the morality of aborting a fetus but live children? No, this is where civilized societies have to draw a line in the sand. Don't we get it that our children are not our possessions? They don't BELONG to us in the same sense that we own our cars and our furniture. So what gives us the right to have them eliminated? And if parents do not have that right, certainly the state does not.

When the law permitting assisted suicide was passed in the Netherlands, opponents of the legislation were dismissed as fanatics for bringing up the old "slippery slope" argument. You know how the argument goes, if you allow doctors or the state to help put a consenting adult to death, what is to keep you from deciding sometime in the future to put persons to death without their consent? If today you give the medical profession the right to put to death kids who suffer from an "extreme deformity" what about mongoloids or marginally retarded babies in the future?

To me this smells too much like murder. The babies will be killed not because they are going to die anyway and we want to ease their pain but because otherwise they will continue to live.

Why get upset over the Netherlands considering this policy? Because, guess what? Taking innocent lives wherever they are in the world diminishes us all. And, if you need to look closer to home, Oregon has an assisted suicide law on its books right now that is strikingly similar to the current law in the Netherlands. As far as I know, Oregon is not considering extending mercy killing to babies or to people who are incapable of making these decisions for themselves, but I am not convinced that the slippery slope cannot become a vertical drop if we are not careful. And if we don't have the humanity in our hearts to be careful of innocent children, may God have mercy on our civilization.

Balkanization of
the Generations

I caught an article in the *New York Times* recently about the major disconnect between the dramatic *decrease* in the number of serious juvenile crimes in this country and the perception on the part of adults, especially older adults, that juvenile crime is totally out of control. The article pointed out that while youth homicides declined by a whopping 68% in the past six years, most Americans believe that juvenile crime is on the rise.

The reason for this disconnect between perception and reality can be blamed, at least in part, on the media's obsession with youth crime. Hardly a night goes by that the six o'clock news is reporting on a mugging or robbery committed allegedly by juvenile delinquents. Never mind that the juveniles involved represent only a miniscule minority of kids. Unfortunately, fear sells almost as well as sex.

But it would be simplistic to place all the blame on the media. I submit that there is another reason for adult's apparent readiness to think the worst of kids. For want of a better term, I call it the Balkanization of the generations.

Reflect for a moment on the fact that an increasing number of older people are choosing to live in retirement communities, where they no longer have to share their streets with the young and support their schools. Even when older people do share the same neighborhoods, kids, parents and grandparents are seldom connected.

Teens may be under the same roof with their parents but they live in their own universe, with their own music, their own set of friends and their own language. Driven by pressure to succeed in an increasingly competitive society, parents inhabit still another world. Neither the younger or the middle generation has much contact with the grandparents. With the possible exception of holidays, the three generations no longer touch one another in any meaningful way. We don't learn from one another because we don't know one another.

Where there is ignorance, there is fear. Old people are afraid of kids because they have no contact with them. The younger generation has its own ignorance and its own fears. For them, the fear is of aging itself. Not knowing older people who are role models of successful aging, young people equate old age with loneliness, physical incapacity and dependence. It scares the hell out of them and, by the way, it does the same to their parents who find themselves getting ever closer to their own "golden age."

I am one old geezer who would like to see my peers take the lead in breaking down the barriers that separate generations from one another. We, after all, are the "elders," the wise ones. It's up to us to set an example for the generations coming after us. Already there are many in the older generation who are reaching out to the young, as mentors, school volunteers and in dozens of ways getting themselves involved with those who will come after them. This is the kind of pro-active role we can play.

Not that breaking down generational walls will be easy, Neither teens nor their parents are waiting with open arms to drink in the wisdom older people have to impart. As a society, we have all bought in to the idea that our value comes from how much money we make or how many toys we possess, from what we "have" or what we "do" rather than who we are. Consequently, the society at large has pretty well written off any contributions that the Medicare generation can make. Like the one time great home run hitter who can no longer catch up with the high hard one, we are perceived as having had our day. So get lost Pops. Big mistake.

We elders should not allow ourselves to be patronized in this way. We do ourselves nor society any favor by allowing it. Life has taught us that in the long run, there is no U-haul truck following the hearse. What matters finally is how we have treated one another and if we have left this world a better place than we found it. That's the kind of wisdom we have to share. If we believe it and live our lives that way, we can be the bridge connecting all three generations.

Loneliness, the Silent Killer

I went to the golf course the other day, by myself, and was paired in short order with three other singles. There was a time when it was difficult to get on a course as a single but no more. It's become a lot easier for singles to go it alone, whether it's golfing or going to the movies or a restaurant. Flying solo is in.

A few years back, I recall reading a book by a Harvard professor entitled *Bowling Alone*. The thesis of the book is that we are fast becoming a nation of single individuals, no longer willing or able to group with others the way we once did.

The author of *Bowling Alone*, a man named Putnam, uses bowling as a symbol of a malaise infecting our society. He points to the fairly recent phenomenon of individuals on their way home from work stopping off at the local bowling alley to bowl a couple of games by themselves. Bowling leagues, which used to make the sport of bowling into a social event, are fast disappearing. Jogging alone or working out at the neighborhood fitness centers are also solitary activities.

To highlight our growing isolation from one another, Putnam also cites the significant decrease in membership being experienced by the Lions, the Rotary and other service clubs. We simply do not band together, whether for a good cause or simply for fun the way we did in the past.

Like it or not, it appears that the Baby Boomer generation, and even more, Generation X'ers are not joiners. It's not that they don't care. Many younger people are generous in their support of worthwhile causes, but their lives are so busy that they would rather make a donation to the Boys and Girls Club than to put their time and energy into organizing a car wash.

When I mentioned some of the points raised in *Bowling Alone* to another single, she put a positive spin on it. "People just feel more self-sufficient these days. They don't have the need (or the time) to join with others."

Maybe she has a point. Twenty years ago there was probably an overemphasis on togetherness. Unless you were part of a couple or a group, you didn't fit in very well. That wasn't cool. On the other hand, there was less isolation and alienation, too. Our human nature has not changed. We are still social animals needing other people.

As we sit alone at our computers or passively in front of the television set, telling the world that we are perfectly content, I wonder if we are kidding ourselves. Bowling alone can be fun. It's simple, doesn't take much time and doesn't cost as much. The problem is you get what you pay for.

The yearning to belong to a family, to a community, a group of friends, is part of being human. It's great that we can live the single life without stigma. It's handy to be able to go to the golf course by yourself or ask for a table for one at the café without embarrassment. But I can't help wondering if all our enthusiasm for living independently may be masking a silent killer in our midst. It's called loneliness.

Dealing With
Compassion Overload

Did you ever get that "I'm on overwhelm, don't bother me feeling?" It hit me big time the other day when looking at the photo of an emaciated little child in the Sudan. In the same magazine was the story of a suicide bombing in Israel causing the death of many innocent people and the picture of two of our young soldiers killed in Iraq.

Who needs this stuff? I thought to myself. I'm just one old guy trying to live in peace. I threw the magazine on the floor and went to the fridge to get myself a beer but the photo of the little kid stuck in my mind. She was about the age of my granddaughter, the healthy, bouncy little girl I had played hide-and-seek with last night. The contrast grabbed hold of me and wouldn't let me go. I wondered if that starving kid in the Sudan had a grandpa.

I have a woman friend who has her own way of dealing with problems that put her on overwhelm. She simply tunes out. A woman in her early 50's, she no longer listens to the news on TV or even reads the daily newspaper. She didn't vote in the last election because "my vote doesn't mean squat." She says she used to get stressed about all this sad news but now realizes that there is nothing she can do about starving children in the Sudan or the war in Iraq or the warming of our planet so she just ignores it all. She told me the other day, with a chuckle, "I've decided that I'm not going to worry my little head about it."

To be polite, I tried to laugh with her but the laugh stuck in my throat. Yet, in a contorted kind of way, I found a part of me envying her. She has found her way of coping and it seems to work. Snuggled up in her own little *"blankie"* of isolation, she has created for herself a sort of neutral zone. There are times when I wish I could do that. Then I remember the words of the Beatles' song that goes "I am a rock. I am an island. And a rock feels no pain and an island never cries." I don't want to be a rock.

Even if I can't solve the problem of hunger in the world, at least I can have the decency to feel compassion for those who are suffering, to listen to the groans of people in pain. Isn't that part of being human? Just because I can't do a lot to alleviate that suffering doesn't mean I can do nothing at all. Cripes, at least I can spare a couple of dollars to send to UNICEF or some other international charity. I am not helpless in the face of human misery. Neither are you.

Few of us are so naïve to think we can change the world but by gosh, we can do something can't we? We don't even have to go to the other side of the world to find families who are impoverished and hungry (Didn't Katrina teach us that?) There are kids in our local community that need mentors and immigrants who need to learn English. The cure for compassion fatigue is not to opt out but to buy in to a solution, one person at a time. We can't do everything but we can do something. As the Jewish saying goes. "He who saves one person saves the world."

He Laughs Well, He's a Good Man

Walking through the park yesterday, I heard one of the purest and sweetest sounds on earth. A little girl feeding bread to the "duckies" was so delighted by the experience that she clapped her hands together and let out a squeal of laughter. To me, there's just something about the laughter of children that reaches me like few other experiences in life. Innocent, spontaneous, a child's laughter, like some magical fountain, seems to bubble up from deep within and cascade down the kid's eyes and cheeks. There is simply no one more alive than a kid laughing. No matter how preoccupied I am with my own concerns, my troubles are forgotten and I, too, have to smile.

While there is something special in a child's laughter, adult laughter can be infectious, too. The great Russian writer, Dostoevsky, once advised young girls in searching for a suitable husband, not to worry unduly about his looks or his wealth. "You'll get better results if you just watch him laugh; if he laughs well, he's a good man."

Maybe Dostoevsky has something. People capable of a good belly laugh (especially at their own expense) probably won't take themselves too seriously. A man with a sense of humor will understand that the world isn't perfect and that folks make mistakes sometimes. Appreciating the comic side of life, they are not apt to get stressed out over little things. A Dad who can laugh at himself won't be too hard on his kids. A husband with a good sense of humor will be easier to live with.

Doctors tell us that the very act of laughing releases the body's natural pain killing endorphins. Laughter relaxes our muscles, makes us feel better about ourselves and our universe. Of all God's creatures, only humans have the ability to laugh. It is a great gift and ours to use in good health throughout our life span. So, even if you are not in the market for a spouse, read a good joke book, watch a funny movie or just observe human nature. There is plenty to laugh at both in yourself and in others. C'mon now. Don't leave all that fun to the kids. How about a big smile?

Kings and Queens
and Common Folks

I ran across an old Italian proverb the other day that tickled me. "Once the game is over, the king and the pawn go back into the same box." Think about that one for a minute.

We humans like to pretend we're better than others of our species. We think we're better because we make more money or wear more fashionable clothes, or have a better education. Maybe, we think we are better because we shop at Nordstrom's instead of Target. (Target shoppers think themselves superior to the Dollar Store patrons.)

Working people look down on welfare folks. The guy who pays cash for his groceries figures that he is better than the person who has to use food stamps.

Teetotalers think they are better than drinkers; social drinkers lord it over alcoholics; the wine connoisseur, sipping his chardonnay, feels several cuts above the beer drinker down at Marty's.

Japanese look down their noses at Koreans; the Brits are uppity with the Irish; Danes feel superior to Swedes; Episcopalians think themselves more enlightened than Baptists.

Young people are prone to think themselves smarter than old folks; slim people look down at fatsos; non smokers like to think they're better than smokers; supervisors have no doubt that they are a cut above the folks they supervise.

On and on it goes. We say that "all men and women are created equal" but, in practice, we keep treating one another as unequal. We separate ourselves into rich and poor, educated or not, "normal" or "abnormal." In a thousand different ways, we insist on denying our equality as human beings.

From time to time, we need to remind ourselves that we all have to put on our pants one leg at a time and that "Once the game is over, the king and the pawn go back into the same box."

The Priest Who Couldn't Cheat

By Hank Mattimore

A REFRESHINGLY HONEST ACCOUNT OF
WHY ONE MAN CHOSE TO LEAVE THE
PRIESTHOOD AND YET REMAIN LOYAL TO
HIS CHURCH

One of nearly 25,000 men in the United States who have
put aside their clerical collars to marry and have a family, Hank Mattimore's
odyssey began in a working class neighborhood of South Buffalo and
included six years as a missionary in Japan and three years as a "honky"
priest in an impoverished black parish in Florida. His journey of faith has a
universality that resonates with the "every man" in each of us.

A copy of *The Priest Who Couldn't Cheat* can be purchased directly from the
author (autographed) by sending $10 including tax and postage to:

> Hank Mattimore
> 2343 Avenida de las Brisas
> Santa Rosa, CA 95405
> 707-544-3763
> hmattimore@yahoo.com

The Priest Who Couldn't Cheat is also available online at **www.amazon.com**